iPad Pro 2020 User Guide

The Complete Beginners and Seniors
Manual to Master the New iPad Pro 4th
Generation and Tips & Tricks for iPadOS

Aaron Madison

Table of Contents

Introduction

There is no doubt that the iPad Pro is Apple's most powerful and advanced tablets. The fourth generation, the 2020 generation, is the latest version available in this range. As you probably know, the iPad Pro 2020 comes in several versions. On the one hand, we have the 11 and 12.9 inches screen, with the only difference being the size. Both in design, processor, capabilities, and other features, both devices are identical. Also, in both, we find two colors: silver and space gray.

On the other hand, we find that, regardless of the screen size, you can buy these iPad Pro in the WiFi version and WiFi + Cellular. The first of these is the traditional model, which will need WiFi networks to connect to the internet. The second of them is a version designed for those who will use the iPad on the go and need a mobile data connection permanently.

The main characteristics for which the new iPad Pro stand out lie in its tremendous power, pushed by the new A12Z Bionic. This is the most powerful processor designed by Apple to date and with substantial differences from the A13 Bionic that the iPhone 11 incorporates. This iPad is capable of carrying out any type of process without problems, such as video, photo, or audio editing.

The screen it incorporates is once again one of the great strengths of this iPad, incorporating a retina panel of the highest quality. As in the previous generation, it has ProMotion technology that allows a refresh rate of 120 Hz. Added to this is a characteristic that is already common in Apple: the TrueTone that allows the brightness and colors of the screen to adjust to the situation we are in and help our eyesight be less damaged.

The double camera that makes its first appearance on an iPad will allow you to take good photos, yes, but it is more intended for the field of Augmented Reality. Apple has been working in this area for years to provide good tools to professionals, but also users. In these new tablets, you can get much more performance thanks to the LiDAR sensor that incorporates a time of flight technology, known as ToF, for its acronym in English.

If it stands out for something, it is also for its software, incorporating all the novelties of iPadOS. This operating system is the great protagonist of all iPad models, and with this one, in particular, you can get much more out of it. From Apple, they are convinced to offer us a perfect hybrid between tablet and computer, increasingly resembling a Mac.

Compatible accessories, such as the new Magic Keyboard that incorporates a keyboard with the trackpad, will delight all users, allowing us to find functionalities dedicated to gestures and navigation through the system through a pointer. This iPad Pro is compatible with the second-generation Apple Pencil, of which we have already verified its good skills in the previous generation.

In any case, it seems that we are facing the best tablet ever created by Apple. Indeed, there is not a profound difference with the previous generation. Still, the new one that it incorporates is very powerful, and it seems that it will satisfy the needs of the most demanding users.

This book will teach you how to use your iPad Pro and optimize performance with the new iPadOS to make your tablet a smart hub and turn it into a mini and smart computer. Learn everything you never imagined was possible with your iPad today. Get your reading glasses let's get started.

CHAPTER ONE

Features of iPad Pro (2020 Model)

Inside, the iPad Pro mounts the Apple A12Z Bionic chip and a quantity of RAM that has not been disclosed, as is the custom at Apple. From the Cupertino company, they affirm that this device is designed for "heavier tasks," such as editing 4K video or making 3D designs. It will be available in two sizes, namely: 11 and 12.9 inches, and its starting price will be 879 euros for the smallest WiFi model.

The usual design, but with more cameras on the back

As far as design is concerned, the main novelties are on the back, since Apple has brought the photographic module of the iPhone 11 Pro to its new iPad Pro (they are two models because there are two sizes, but we will talk about them in singular). This module has been placed in the upper left corner and, effectively, houses two cameras: an angle with two magnifications, a wide-angle. We will talk about them later.

On the upper edge, we have two speakers, three microphones, and the start button. At the bottom, two speakers and the USB Type-C port. On the left edge, another microphone and on the right edge, the volume buttons, the magnetic connector to charge the Apple Pencil, the Smart Connector for the keyboard, and, on the case of 4G models, the slot for nanoSIM.

As for the screen, Apple stretches the panel to the corners, although it retains small edges on all sides. As we said, the iPad Pro comes in 11 or 12.9 inches, and the differences are in the resolution. In the 11-inch model, we talk about 2,388 pixels x 1,688 pixels, while the 12.9-inch model amounts to 2,732 x 2,048 pixels. In both cases, we found 264 pixels per inch, 120Hz refresh rate, P3 color space, an oleophobic and anti-reflective coating, and 600 nits of brightness.

LiDAR scanner and trackpad support

Known on the outside, let's see what the new iPad Pro offers inside. Apple, as always happens, has not revealed the amount of RAM, but the processor will be the Apple A12Z Bionic, a 64-bit chip with Neural Engine and the M12 co-processor. The two models share internal storage; that is, they can be obtained with 128, 256, or 512 GB and reach up to 1TB of memory. No 64GB version.

The innovations are at the operating system level since with the arrival of iPadOs 13.4 comes the support for the trackpad, thus bringing the experience of using an iPad Pro closer to that of a laptop. Apple highlights that this support is not exactly like in MacOS, but that the pointer will highlight the elements in the interface. The trackpad will be compatible with multitouch gestures. The launch of the iPad Pro (2020) has also been used to launch a Magic Keyboard with a trackpad.

As for the LiDAR scanner, Apple explains that the component is capable of measuring the distance to surrounding objects up to five meters away, both indoors and outdoors. The iPad combines the LiDAR sensor, camera data, and motion sensors to interpret better scenes, something designed for augmented reality applications.

The device does not have a fingerprint reader, but, like the iPhone, it has Face ID for facial unlocking. There is no lack of connectivity either, as the new iPad Pro lands with WiFi 6, Bluetooth 5.0, USB

Type-C port, and 4G connectivity option. No headphone jack.

Taking inspiration from iPhone 11 for cameras

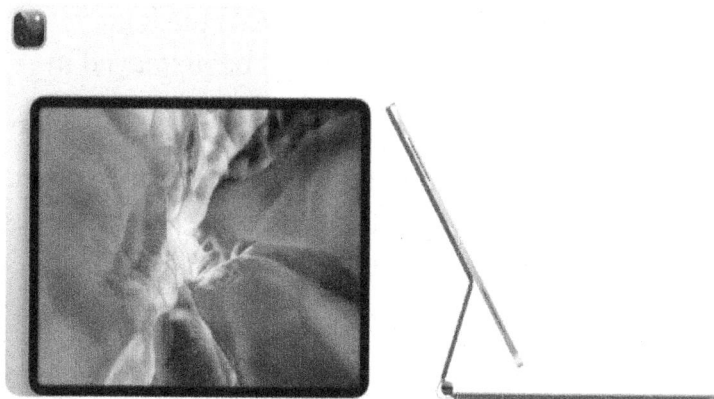

Apple has followed the path marked by the iPhone 11 and has brought neither more nor less than two cameras to the back of its new tablet. They do not share resolution, but they do configure lenses.

Both models share the main 12-megapixel lens with f / 1.8 aperture with two-magnification optical zoom and up to five digital magnifications and a second wide-angle lens with 125º field of view, 10 megapixels, and f / 2.4 aperture and a third lens. Highlights include Smart HDR and 4K 60FPS recording with wide-angle and standard wide-angle. Selfies are at hand with a seven-megapixel TrueDepth sensor with f / 2.2 aperture.

How to Set Up iPad

- Press and hold the power button on the device until you see the Apple logo.
- **"Hello,"** greetings will be displayed in several languages. You can activate VoiceOver or Zoom from the greeting screen if you have any visual impairment.
- Choose your language. Next, touch your country or region. This affects the way information is presented on your device, for example, date, time, contacts, and other content. In this instance, you can touch the blue accessibility button to configure **Accessibility Options** that can optimize the configuration experience and use of the new device.
- If you have another iPadOS device running on iPadOS 12, 13, or later, you can use it to configure your new device automatically using **Quick Start**.
- If you do not have another device running iOS 12, 13, or later, touch "**Set up Manually**" to continue.
- You must connect to a Wi-Fi network, a cellular network, or iTunes to activate your iPad and continue configuring it.
- Touch the Wi-Fi network you want to use or select another option. If you set up an iPad (Wi-Fi + Cellular), you may need to insert your SIM card first.

- You can opt to configure Face ID or Touch ID. Touch **Continue** and follow the instructions, or tap "**Set up Later in Settings**."
- Next, create a six-digit code for privacy. A code is needed to use features such as Face ID, Touch ID, and Apple Pay. If you prefer a four-digit code, a custom passcode, or don't have a passcode, tap "**Passcode Options**."
- If you have an iCloud or iTunes backup or an Android device, you can restore or transfer your data from the previous device to the new device.
- If you do not have a backup or other device, choose **Set Up as New Device** option.
- Input your Apple ID and password, or select "**Forgot password or don't have an Apple ID?**" From here, you can recover your Apple ID or your password, create an Apple ID or set it up later. If you use more than one Apple ID, touch "**Use different Apple IDs for iCloud and iTunes?**"
- When you log in with your Apple ID, you may be asked for a verification code that you will receive from the previous device.
- On the following screens, you can decide if you want to share information with app developers and allow iPadOS to update automatically.

- You will then be asked to configure or activate services and functions, such as Siri.
- If you're logged in with your Apple ID, follow prompt to set up Apple Pay and the iCloud keychain.
- Also, you can set up Screen Time to monitor the amount of time your kids spend on the tablet. Follow onscreen instructions to set up other features if needed.
- Finally, click on "**Get Started**" to begin using your iPad.

How to Update your iPad

If you want to update your iPad to the new iPadOS, you only have to go to the **Settings** section, enter **General** and click on **Software Update**. On this screen, you will see your update ready and you can start its download and installation. You can also do an installation from scratch to leave the device as new, restoring your iPad, and then looking for the update.

Backup your iPad on macOS Catalina

To create a local iPad backup file connected to your Mac, which contains (among other things) all your settings, files, and application data, follow the steps below.

- Connect your iPad to your Mac using a Lighting cable.
- Open a new Finder window by clicking on the desktop, then select the File menu and choose the New Finder Window command (or press Command - N on the keyboard).
- Now click on your device in the Finder sidebar, it appears below the Locations heading.
- If a message requests your device password or to Trust this computer, simply follow the steps on the screen and tap **Trust**.
- Click through the content categories at the top of the window to select the media files you want to sync to your iPad.
- To back up all the local data on your iPad to your Mac, tap the option "**back up all the data on your iPad to this Mac**."
- To encrypt the backup, choose the option underneath, and set a password.
- You can view more options allowing you to personalize how you sync and backup. For example, having the "**automatically**

sync" option toggled on means it'll backup and sync every time you plug it in.

- Tap the "**backup now**" button to manually back up your iPad.
- Lastly, tap "**Apply**" at the bottom, and your iPad data and settings will be backed up physically to your Mac device.

Restore your iPad on macOS Catalina

To restore your iPad from a backup stored on your Mac, do the following:

- First, connect your iPad to a Mac with macOS Catalina 10.15+.
- Open a new Finder window by clicking on the desktop, then select the File menu and choose the New Finder Window command or press Command - N on the keyboard.
- Click on the device in the Finder sidebar just below the Locations heading.
- You may need to click Pair if this is the first time you connect this device to this Mac.
- In the Backup section, click on the **Restore Backup** button .
- Look at the date and size of each backup and choose the most relevant ones, then click on **Restore**.

- Wait for the restoration time to end, which can take between a few seconds and an hour or more, depending on the size of the backup file and the speed of your computer and device, and other factors. If prompted, enter the password for your encrypted backup.

Restore from iCloud Backup

When you're initially setting up your iPad for the first time, you'll get the prompt to restore from backup.

- When you get to the "**App & Data**" page, tap **Restore from iCloud Backup**.
- Enter the Apple ID and password you are using for iCloud, then tap **Next**.
- The terms of use will be displayed. Tap **Agree**.
- A list of backups stored in iCloud appears with the name of the device and the date the backup was taken. In addition to iPad backup, you can also choose from backups of other devices such as iPad.
- When you select a backup, the settings will be restored.
- When restoration of settings is completed, and the home screen is displayed,

restoration of apps, photos, ringtones, etc. will begin.

Turn On iCloud Backup

This is done automatically once a day as long as you set it. Key content is backed up, but not all.

iCloud can use up to 5GB for free. If there is not enough space, change the storage plan from the iPad settings app.

- Open the **Settings** app
- Next, tap **your name** at the top of the display.
- Then tap **iCloud**.
- A list of iCloud functions will be displayed. Tap **iCloud Backup**.
- If iCloud Backup is off, turn it on.
- Turning on iCloud backup turns off automatic backup via iTunes
- When **iCloud Backup** is turned on, the backup via iTunes that is automatically performed when the iPad is connected to the computer is turned off.
- Since iCloud backups and iTunes automatic backups cannot be used together, it is usually a good idea to use iCloud backups and regularly back up manually with iTunes.

- Tap **Create backup now** to start back up on the spot. A Wi-Fi environment is required, but it is not necessary to connect to a power source.
- The backup is complete when the message **"Creating backup"** disappears, and the time of the previous backup is displayed.

Turn Off iCloud Auto Sync for Photos and Videos

Photos and videos taken with an iPad are automatically uploaded to iCloud.

Because this option is turned on by default, you may unknowingly consume a large amount of data and limit the speed. You need to change the setting to turn off the feature.

- Launch the **Settings** app on your iPad
- Select "**Photos**" on the setting screen
- Proceed to "**Mobile Data Communication**"
- Switch off "**Mobile Data Communication**"

How to Reset iPad

- From the home screen, tap **Settings** > **General**, then tap **Reset** at the bottom of the "**General**" screen.
- Tap **Erase iPad** and confirm.

How to Create a New Apple ID

- Open the **Settings** app.
- Click on Sign in to your iPad at the upper part of the screen.
- Tap "**Don't have an Apple ID.**"
- Next, tap **Create Apple ID**.

- Enter your birthday, then tap "**Next**" at the top right of the screen.
- Now enter your name and press "**Next**."
- Choose your "**existing email address**" or opt to "**get a free iCloud address**."

⟨ Back

Email Address

Use your current email address ›

Get a free iCloud email address ›

- Input your email address and then click "**Next**.".
- Now create a password eight characters long and click "**Next**.". Your password will have to include at least one uppercase letter and at least one numerals to go through.
- You will receive a text message or call to confirm your identity, tap **Continue**.
- Agree to the terms and conditions.
- Enter your iPad Passcode, if it has one.
- Choose whether you want a confirmation email sent to the email address you enter or different.
- Enter the verification code from your email to your iPad.
- Tap **Merge**.

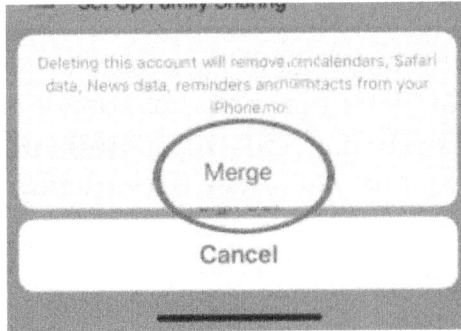

Deleting this account will remove calendars, Safari data, News data, reminders and contacts from your iPhone.

Merge

Cancel

- That's all, from here you can adjust the payment and shipping information, set up iTunes and App Store, set up Family Sharing, and more.

Change Apple ID on the iPad

- To log in with another Apple ID on your iOS device, navigate to the **Settings** app.
- Tap on **your name** above. At the top of the screen, you can view the Apple ID you're logged in with. Scroll down and touch "**Sign out**."
- Next, you will be required to enter your Apple ID and authorize your entry. In the following screen, you can select which information should be saved in the iCloud. To make a copy, you move the slider to the right; then, you tap again on "**Sign out**."
- Once your former Apple ID has been erased, you can now sign up again. Go into your settings and tap on "**Sign in to**

iPad." Now you can enter the e-mail address and password for your other Apple ID.

Set Up Apple Pay

With Apple Pay, you can conveniently use contactless services in shops, such as the discount store, in restaurants, hotels, or at the gas station; pay with the iPad, directly and without entering a PIN. This usually applies to amounts below a certain figure. For payments exceeding this maximum amount, it is usually necessary to enter the PIN for security reasons. By the way, if you use Apple Pay, you will not incur any costs. As with credit card payments, the respective dealer takes over the fees, so that the service is free for you.

Contactless payment is made possible by the NFC transmission standard, which allows the exchange of data over short distances. You can use Apple Pay wherever you see the following signs:

Configure Apple Pay on the iPad

Method 1: Settings app

- Go to the **Settings** app.
- Touch "**Wallet & Apple Pay**"

- Next, tap "**Add Cards**."
- No matter which of the two ways you choose: After an info screen on the Apple Pay function, which you skip to "**Continue**" with a tip, you have the ability to scan your bank or credit card. The card number and your name will be taken over automatically. Alternatively, you can enter the card information manually.
- With a tip on "**Next**" in the top right, you jump to the next step. Your card will then be verified by the respective bank or card issuer. Once the verification is done, tap on "**Next**," and you can use Apple Pay on your iPad. Your card or cards are deposited directly in the Wallet app on the iPad.
- You can add up to 12 cards. If you use multiple cards with Apple Pay, you can choose a preferred card by using the Wallet app. In the event that your default card is not accepted in a particular store, you can easily pay with another card via Apple Pay.

Method 2: Wallet app

- Go to **Wallet App** on your iPad
- Tap the blue **Plus icon** in the top left corner of the home screen.
- Touch **Add Cards** to choose the card that you want to add.

CHAPTER TWO

Show Previews on the Lock Screen

- Launch the **Settings** app.
- Next, select "**Messages.**"
- Touch **Show previews**.
- In the next submenu, you can now choose one of three options: "**Always,**" "**If Unlocked,**" or "**Never.**" Tap on "**Always,**" so that a small blue hook appears behind it. Then you can leave the settings again, and you will receive the messages directly as before without having to unlock the device.

How to Use a Wireless or USB Mouse

Make sure that Bluetooth is turned on and that you have not paired the mouse you want to use with another device.

- Open the **Settings** app.
- Scroll down and tap **Accessibility**.
- Look under the "**Physical & Motor**" section and then click on "**Touch.**"

- In the menu toggle on "**Assistive Touch.**"
- And from here, you simply connect your mouse to your device. This should start immediately.

Tips for Using the Mouse

You can move the cursor the seconds you connect the mouse, but the cursor itself is a large, gray circle designed to imitate a fingerprint. The only way to change that is to make it bigger and change the color. It's not impossible to achieve the same precision you get with a desktop cursor, but that takes practice.

By default, the **AssistiveTouch** circular menu remains on the screen while **AssistiveTouch** is on, although you can move it across the screen with your finger. Usually, you also activate the

AssistiveTouch menu by right-clicking. However, to hide the menu, you can go to "**Settings > Accessibility > Tap> AssistiveTouch**" and "**Always show menu.**"

If you do not change the settings, the menu is always displayed when right-clicking.

Customize the Buttons on the Mouse

Go to **Settings > Utilities > Tap > AssistiveTouch > Pointing Devices**, and then select your connected mouse.

Customize AssistiveTouch

Assistive touch is a great accessibility feature in iOS devices. With this feature, you can perform arrays of gestures like pinch, multi-finger swipe, 3D touch, Pointing Devices, Mouse Keys etc. An important thing is while you've turned on the Assistive Touch, the iOS device at the time doesn't require pressing any physical button either the home button or the power and volume buttons. Double-tap the Assistive touch to display the App Switcher.

- Take a screenshot on iPad without Side buttons by bringing up the Screenshot feature on the main menu of Assistive Touch.

- You can add gestures to the Assistive Touch Menu such as Home, Notification, Lock Screen, 3D Touch, and more. Tap the plus icon "+" to add the other settings to Assistive Touch.
- Launch the "**Settings**" app.
- Scroll down and select "**Accessibility**."
- Tap "**Touch**"
- Go to the "**AssistiveTouch**." Turn on **AssistiveTouch** to wake up on the home screen and use it like the Virtual Home button as well.
- Select "**Customize Top-Level Menu**."
- And if you don't like the customizations that you have made in Assistive Touch, then tap "**Reset**" on the same screen to revert the process.
- When you get back to **Touch Menu**, you will be allowed to set Custom Actions, like what will happen when you Single-Tap, Double-Tap and Long-Press the **Assistive Touch**. Open section one by one and make a selection.
- Note: All these options are available in Single-Tap, Double-Tap, and Long-Press custom actions in Assistive Touch.
- Keep in mind that when you "**Reset All Settings**," on iPad, all the customized assistive touch settings will clear to default. You have to customize them again or else use them as it is.

How to Use the QuickTake Feature

To switch from shooting photos to capturing a video has been made easier with the QuickTake video shortcut on iPad 11 series cameras. Here are the steps to use the QuickTake video shortcut on your iPad 11 series:

- Open the **Camera** app
- Press and hold the shutter button

- Let go to end recording a video
- Swipe to the lock icon to continue to record the video

- Tap the red icon to end and save your video
- The other alternative if you need to keep recording a video without holding the shutter button down is to simply swipe toward the lock icon. If you do that, you'll likewise get the shutter button to snap still images while you're recording.
- If you used the video lock alternative, tap the red square to stop recording and save your video.

How to Use the New Camera App

Here's a list of what's new in the iPad Pro Camera app and how to use it.

Zoom in and out of the iPad

The camera zoom control has been changed on the iPad 11 series camera. If you have an iPad 11, there are two buttons: .5x and 1x. .5x is the new ultrawide camera, and 1x is the standard camera. On iPad 11 Pro and Pro Max, there's a third button for 2x zoom.

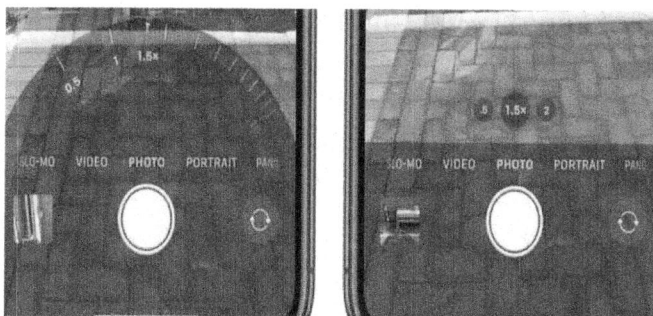

You can tap the button to jump to that zoom level. However, you can also move these buttons horizontally to open a zoom wheel. This allows you to select zoom levels and display the appropriate focal length in 35 mm movies. You can also pinch and zoom with two fingers to adjust the zoom and switch between lenses. The focal length wheel is not displayed.

Record Videos Quickly

To quickly record a video, make sure the camera mode is set to Photo. If you then press the shutter button for a long time, the red recording light comes on. The video is being recorded.

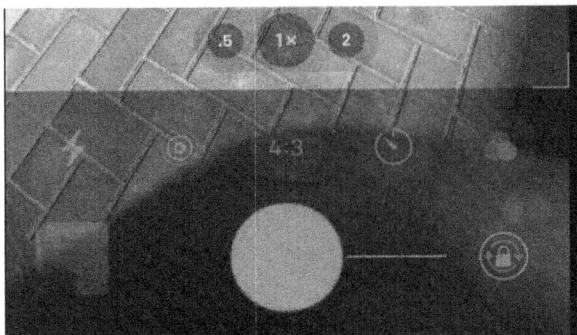

If you remove your finger from the screen, the video ends. If you want to continue recording without holding your finger, simply drag the red trigger to the lock icon on the right side of the screen. This locks the video and displays a default stop button that you can touch as you like.

How to take burst pictures

Pressing and holding the trigger in the iPad Pro series now activates QuickTake, which lets you quickly capture video without leaving the photo mode. Here's the new gesture for using burst mode.

- Press the shutter-release button, and then quickly pull to the left toward the thumbnail stack of photos to take a series.

(If the shutter button stays red, you have pressed your finger too long, and the tablet thinks you want to record a video, stop it and start over.)

- The trigger circle moves with your finger to indicate that the series has started, and the displayed number indicates the current number of photos in the series. When your burst is finished, simply release your finger from the screen to exit.

How to take night photos

- When the scene is really dark, the night mode is automatically activated by the camera, and in the upper left corner of the screen, a yellow night mode icon is displayed, indicating the number of seconds the photo takes to take the picture. To turn off night mode, simply tap the button to turn it off.
- If the scene is lit with low to medium light, the Night Mode option is visible but not activated (not highlighted in yellow).

29

If you think that the photo would benefit from night mode, you can manually tap to turn it on. You can also drag the slider to adjust the exposure time.

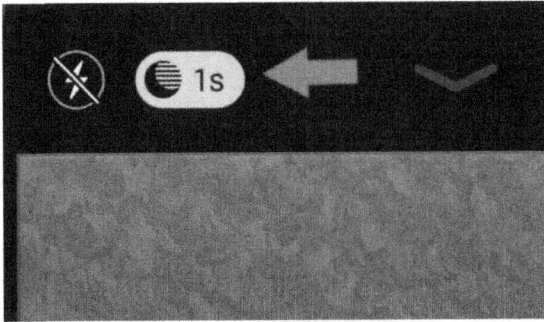

- When you're done with active night mode, tap the shutter button and hold the tablet steady for the assigned duration. It will create a brighter picture and gather as much detail as possible over the 3 to 5 second period.

Change image detail and aspect ratio

- The iPad Pro camera has a hidden drawer with additional controls. If you notice an upward-pointing triangle arrow, swipe up in the viewfinder to display the new drawer with the controls.
- There are more sophisticated options for flash, night mode, live photos, cropping, timer, and filters. You may have noticed that the square camera has been removed from the main wheel interface. You can

take square photos instead by changing
the aspect ratio in this drawer.

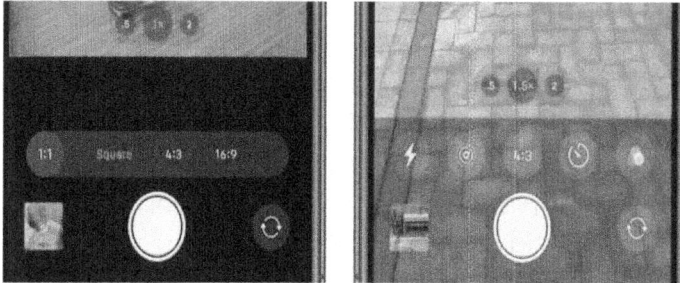

- Change the aspect ratio by tapping the
  button (which is set to 4: 3 by default).
  Then tap on Square. There are options for
  Square (1: 1), 4: 3, and 16: 9. You can
  customize the crop later at any time when
  editing the image in the Photo Library.

How to take square photos

To take square photos, follow the flows below:

- Open the **Camera** app
- At the top center of the screen, touch the
  ^ icon (or swipe up in the viewfinder).
- Tap 4: 3 (this is the default)
- Now choose **square**
- Take pictures. Follow the same steps to
  take pictures with an aspect ratio of 16: 9:

Activate"Capture Outside the Frame"

When you take pictures or videos utilizing either the wide lens or telephoto lens point, the camera will, at the same time, shoot or record utilizing the next widest sensor. So the wide lens is enabled when you shoot with the telephoto lens, and the ultra-wide is enabled when you shoot with the wide.

- With this feature active, you can take your shot, tap **Edit** in the preview window, tap the **Crop tool**, and select **Straighten**.

- You'll have the option to utilize the area captured outside the frame of the photograph.

Apple has disabled it by default for photographs, so you'll have to turn it on.

- Go to **Settings** > **Camera** > **Composition** and see the three switches.

Outside the frame, there are separate **photo and video capture functions**, and a setting called **Auto Apply**.

- If out of frame recording is enabled, you should be able to switch to the photo app after taking a photo or video and use the Crop tool to extend the edges of the frame. The **Apply Automatically** option does this on your behalf when detecting cropped faces or similar automatic composition changes.

Auto Low-Light FPS

This video feature can be used when recording in either 1080P 30 FPS or 4K 30 FPS. To check this feature is turned on for your device, open **Settings > Camera > Record Video** and ensure the **Auto Low-Light FPS** toggle is enabled.

If you don't use the auto low-light option, the iPad will still record video in extended dynamic range, almost like applying HDR to video capture, all the way up to the maximum 4K 60 FPS format.

Using the Ultra Wide Camera

One of the great innovations in the iPad 11 series is an ultra-wide camera that allows users to capture a much wider field of view without the need for an external lens. Continue reading on how to use the ultra-wide camera on the iPad 11

and iPad 11 Pro, including manually entering
your focal length.

The iPad 11 and iPad 11 Pro have a new camera
app with exclusive features such as night mode, a
new user interface for the new ultra-wide-angle
lens, and more.

With the ultra-wide-angle camera of the iPad 11,
it should be noted that no optical image
stabilization (OIS) is installed, as in the case of
the wide-angle camera and the telephoto camera.
The more stable your iPad can be when using the
ultra-wide-angle lens, the better the results will
be. The night mode does not work with the ultra-
wide-angle camera.

The ultra-wide-angle camera of the latest iPads
has a 120-degree field of view, an f2.4 aperture,
and a 5-element lens.

Using the Ultra Wide Camera:

- Open the **Camera** app
- Tap "**0.5**" just above the shutter button to
  switch to the ultra-wide camera.
- Keep your iPad steady and take pictures
- Alternatively, you can hold down a zoom
  button such as "**1**" or "**0.5**" to manually
  select a focal length between the default
  settings.
- If you want to fine-tune the focal length
  for your shot, hold down one of the zoom
  buttons and slide it up or down.

CHAPTER THREE

Customize Text Message Tones

Each iPad comes with many text tones. You can make one to be your default text tone. Each time you get a text message, the default tone will sound.

Change the default text tone by navigating through the process below:

- Go to the **Settings** app.
- Tap **Sounds & Haptics**.
- Tap **Text Tone**.
- Swipe to browse the list of text tones (you can utilize ringtones as text tones; they're on this screen, as well). Tap a tone to hear it play.
- When you've discovered the text tone you need to utilize, tap it to put a checkmark by it. Your decision is automatically saved, and that tone is set as your default.

Turn on Dark Mode

- To activate, simply head to **Settings**
- Tap **Display & Brightness**
- Choose **Dark**.

Set Wallpapers that Reacts to Dark Mode

- To set a dynamic color-shifting wallpaper, go to the **Settings** app
- Select **Wallpapers**
- Tap **Choose a New Wallpaper > Stills**. Wallpapers that react to Dark Mode changes are marked with a small, **bisected circle** in the bottom-right, and have a line down the middle of the image to show the changes you can expect.
- If you fancy to retain your personalized wallpaper, go back to the **Wallpaper** options, and toggle the option for **Dark Appearance Dims Wallpaper**. While your wallpaper won't change like reacting wallpapers, it will dim it slightly, so any lighter areas won't dazzle while Dark Mode is active.

Set Your Notification Preferences

You can pick whether to show an app notification's on the lock screen or if you'd only like it shown when your face has been recognized.

To customize this feature, go to **Settings > Notifications > Show Previews** to choose how content is or isn't shown on the lock screen, alternatively, go to **Settings > Notifications** to adjust the lock screen look.

Set Messages to Share your Personalized Contact Data

New to iOS 13 is the option to create your very own contact photo and name to be displayed on other people's iPad device. You can pick whether this is enabled for just contacts or everyone; however, they have the last say on whether they acknowledge your chosen information.

Tap **Settings > Messages > Share Name & Photo** where you can configure these and whom this automatically gets shared with.

Turn on Text, Call, and FaceTime forwarding

For calls, go to **Settings > Phone > Calls on Other Devices**, and toggle on the switch for the devices you'd like to get calls on. It's almost the same for messages and FaceTime, also. **Settings > Messages > Text Message Forwarding** gets you to similar toggles for messaging.

Filter Unknown Calls and Messages

You can have messages from unknown senders silenced and arranged into a separate list in your inbox for further review.

- For calls, go to **Settings > Phone > Silence Unknown Callers** and toggle the switch on to filter calls, or **Settings > Messages > Filter Unknown Senders** for message filtering.

Set Location Preferences

Apps

- To enable this feature go **to Settings.**
- Tap "**Privacy.**"

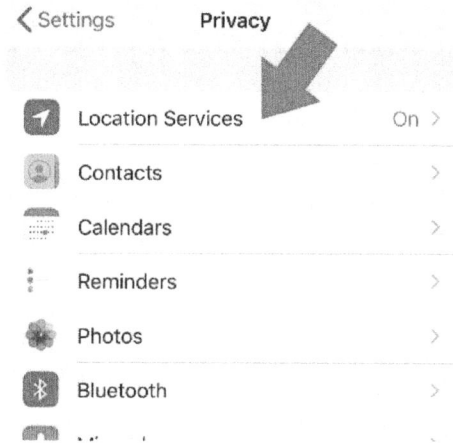

- Select "**Location Services,**" to set a general rule for all apps, or go into each app and select "Never," "Always," while utilizing the app, or "ask next time."
- The last option will prompt your iPad to ask you each time an app requests to access your location data.

Set Filming Speed

- Go to **Settings**
- Tap on **Camera**
- Tap **Record Video**

- Next, pick your favorite filming speed.

Turn Off Required Attention on Face ID

- Go to **Settings**
- Tap **Face ID & Passcode**
- Select **Require Attention for Face ID** and switch the toggle off.

Format to Store Pictures & Videos

- Go to **Settings.**
- Tap **Camera.**
- Tap **Formats**.

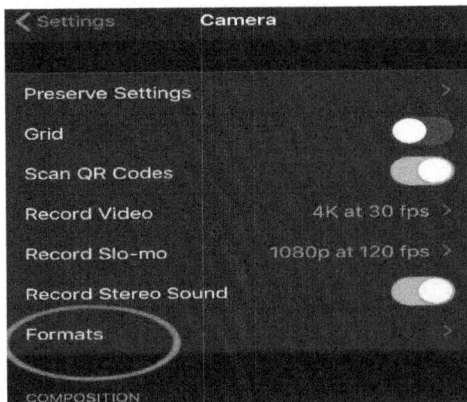

- Choose **Most Compatible** rather than
  High Efficiency.

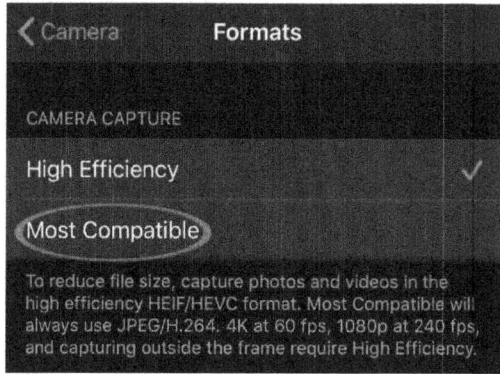

Very simple, isn't it?

How to Enable iCloud
Keychain on iPad

You can use this feature to access your saved
logins and passwords, credit card information,
and personal details. First, you'll need to enable
it.

- Open the **Settings** app
- Tap your **Apple ID banner**.
- Select **iCloud**.
- Scroll down and press **Keychain**.
- Turn on the **iCloud Keychain** switch.
- Input your Apple ID password if
  prompted.

- If this is your first time, you will be asked to create a password. You also have the option to verify it with another device. Next, if you resolve to complete your account, you'll be ready to store information more securely on your iPad.

How to Access iCloud Keychain Passwords

- Open **Safari**
- In the menu bar, click "**Safari.**"
- Next, tap "**Preferences.**"
- Look for "**Passwords**" along the top. Here you'll see a list of passwords and login details for all web pages. Apple will notify you if you've recycled the same password on numerous web pages, and provide a swift link to change your password on a service's website.
- You can freely copy and paste the different usernames and passwords, and AirDrop them to other devices.

How to Activate Siri

- Head to **Settings**
- Tap **Siri & Search** > **Listen** to enable the feature.
- After you've enabled Siri, just say the command "**Hey Siri**" to activate the voice assistant.

Activate Siri with Side Button

To activate Siri, press and hold the Side button for a few seconds (two to three) will be okay.

How to Exit Siri

When you're done with Siri, and you want to exit, simply swipe up from the bottom of the screen or press the side button to return to the home screen.

Change Siri's language

- Go to **Settings**
- Swipe down and tap **Siri & Search**
- Select **Language**
- Pick a new language and tap **Change Language** to confirm your selection
- Tap the "**Hey Siri**" toggle on **Siri & Search** settings page to train Siri on the new language.

CHAPTER FOUR

Change iPad's Language

- On the Home screen, go to **Settings**.
- Next, tap **General**.
- Scroll down and select **Language & Region**.
- On the following screen, choose "**iPad Language**."
- Select your language from the rundown.
- A notification will require you to confirm the new language. Press the first option.
- After your iPad updates the preferred language, it should automatically be showing the language you choose.

Set Up Optimized Battery Charging

- Go to **Settings**
- Tap **Battery**
- Select **Battery Health** and turn on "**Optimized Battery Charging**."

How to Use the New Scroll Bar

When you're scrolling a webpage in Safari, a new Scroll Bar shows up on the right side of the screen. Only instead of just being a handy way to see where you're at on a page, you can now use it to scroll faster.

Try it out by starting to scroll on a page, then long-press on the scroll bar and drag it up or down. The faster you drag, the faster Safari will scroll.

How to Scan Documents in the Files App

- Open the **Files app**, select the **Browse** tab, tap on the three-dot icon in the top-right corner, then **Scan Documents**.
- Hold your device over the document you want to scan, and it should automatically capture the page.
- You can scan multiple pages into one PDF file and then save it to iCloud or import it into another app once you're done.

Share Photos Without Location Information

- To see how this works, select an image(s) you want to share in the Photos app, then touch on **Options** at the top of the screen and turn off **Location** under the part labeled "**Include**."

Delete Apps from the Notification Screen

When you see an app you want to do away within the Updates list, simply swipe to the left across the listing and then tap **Delete** to erase the app from your device.

Remove App Size Limitations on Cellular Data

Go to **Settings > iTunes & App Store > App Downloads** to get rid of the limit or have the App Store ask you if you want to download any apps over 200MB.

How to Take Long Screenshots of Websites

With this feature you no longer have to take multiple screenshots of a webpage in order to capture the text of an article, iOS 13's screenshot tool has a new tactic.

- Launch Safari and visit any website you want to take a screenshot.

- Next, take just one screenshot of the website and instantly tap on the thumbnail preview.

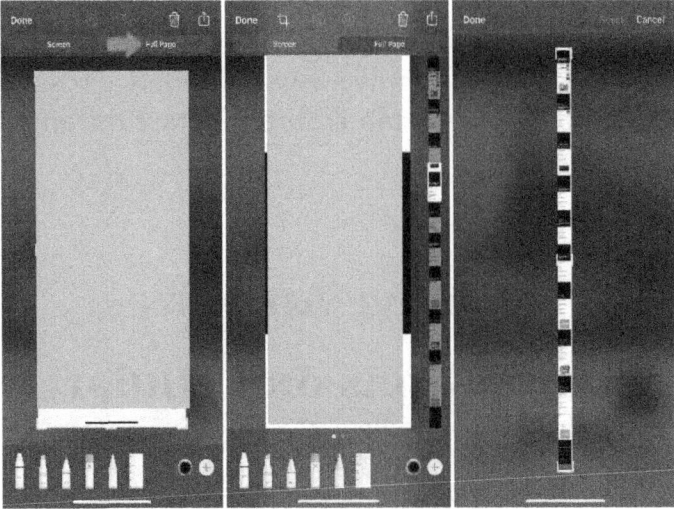

- Above the screenshot, there are two options: **Screen** and **Full Page**.
- Selecting **Full Page** will turn the entirety of the webpage you're viewing into a PDF file that you can then crop, annotate and save to the Files app.

Customize Notification Centre

- Go to **Settings**
- Select **Notifications**.

- Touch **Show Previews** at the upper part of the Notifications screen.
- Choose **"Always,"** **"When,"** **"Unlocked,"** or **"Never"** and tap **"Back"** at the top of the screen to go back to the Notifications screen.
- Touch one or more of the apps on the display.
- Push the slider next to **Allow Notifications** to the **ON** position.
- Touch the circle under **Notification Center** to check it, and notifications from the app begin to display in the **Notification Center**. Alternatively, you can also select **Lock Screen** if you want notifications to appear on your lock screen and **Banner** if you want them to appear at the top of the screen.
- Repeat this process for every other app you wish to post to Notification Center.

Customize Widgets in Notification Center

- Open the **Notification Center** by pulling down from the top left corner of the screen.

- Swipe through from left to right in area that is not an alert to display the "Today view."
- Scroll to the bottom of the **Today view** and tap **Edit** to adjust which apps are noticeable.

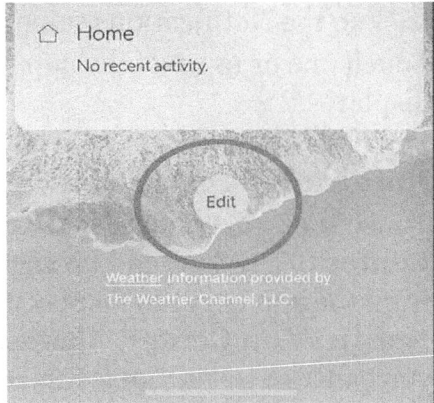

- In the screen that opens is a rundown of the considerable number of widgets right now accessible on the iPad. Tap the **minus** on the red button next to every widget you need to remove from the Today screen. Drag the three-line handle next to a widget to reorder the rundown.
- Scroll down to the **More Widgets** segment, which contains widgets that are accessible however not activated in the Today screen. Tap the **plus sign** in a green button next to any widget you need to activate.

How to Switch Apps

- Touch your finger to the gesture area at the bottom of the iPad 11 display.
- Swipe from left to right to go to the former app.
- To return to the next app, swipe from right to left.
- Note, in the event that you stop or get interrupted, the last app you were on turns into the recent app so you can just swipe back from it, not forward anymore.

Display Multitasking Quick App Switcher

- Touch your finger to the gesture area at the bottom of the iPad 11 display.
- Swipe up slightly. (Try not to flick. Simply keep your finger on the screen until you get a short far up, the pull away.)

Force Quit Apps

- Touch your finger to the gesture area at the extreme bottom of the iPad 11 display.
- Swipe up slightly.

- Pause. Try not to lift your finger up right away. (That will take you Home.)
- Lift up your finger.
- Swipe up on an app card. Boom! It's gone.
- When you're in a killing mode, you can remove as many apps as you wish.

How to Access Reachability Mode

- Open **Settings** from the Home screen.
- Tap on **General**.
- Tap on **Accessibility**.
- Switch **Reachability** to ON.

How to Access Control Center

- Touch your finger to the gesture area at the extreme bottom of the iPad 11 display.
- Swipe down.
- Once more, you can even swipe down from the top right of **Reachability** to access **Control Center**.

Share Music over AirPods

Apple has never liked to perform complex processes, so enabling this new feature is very easy.

You will have to pair the new pair of headphones with your device before you can send music. To sync a friend's AirPods or PowerBeats Pro, the same process is done to match yours. If you no longer remember how it is done, we explain how:

- Place the pair of AirPods or PowerBeats Pro of guests in their carrying case.
- Open the **Settings** app and tap on the Bluetooth menu.
- Press and hold the pairing button on the back of the charging case.
- Play the other set of headphones when they appear on **Other devices**.
- That is all you need to do. To make sure everything is set up correctly, turn on your own and your friend's headphones and make sure they both appear as Connected in the device list.
- When you're ready to start playing music, make sure both devices are connected. You can also see both sets of headphones in the AirPlay configuration, where you can also set separate volumes for each pair.

CHAPTER FIVE

Set Up Monthly Cycle Data

- Launch **Health App** on your iPad. Under the **Browse** tab, select the **Cycle Tracking** option from the rundown.

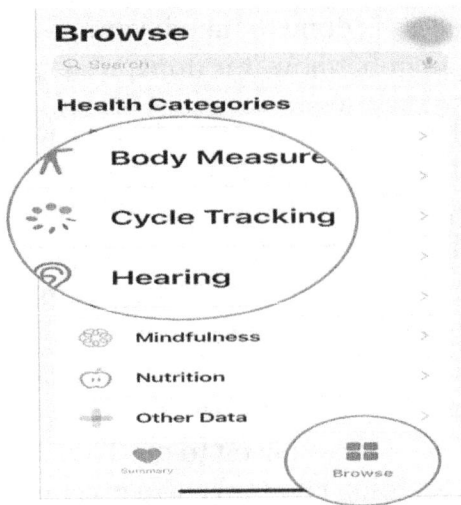

- Next, tap on **Get Started,** and now you'll be asked with specific questions, for example, when did your former period start? How long does your period normally last? How long is your regular cycle? And so forth. Enter every one of the information you know and tap on "**Next**" or tap on "**I Don't Know**" to continue. This will set up essential monthly cycle information on your iPad.

- If you need to edit the period length, just tap on **Options** directly beside **Cycle Log** and adjust the **period length** according to your cycle.

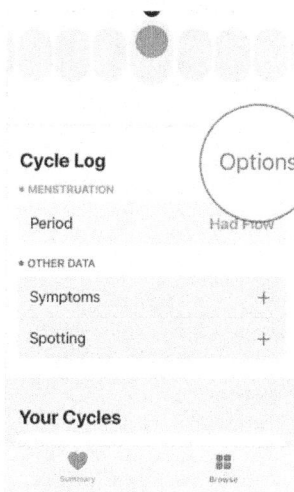

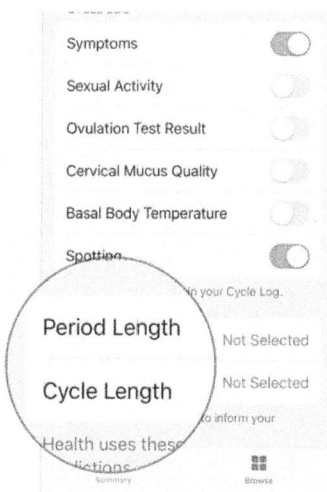

Make sure that every information is accurate as this will be used by the Health App to predict fertility schedule and period predictions. However, you can change the information as the month passes on the grounds that not all cycle is constant.

Customize Cycle Tracking Options

- Launch the **Health App** and head over to the **Cycle Tracking** option by scrolling down. Tap on **Options** directly beside **Cycle Log**.

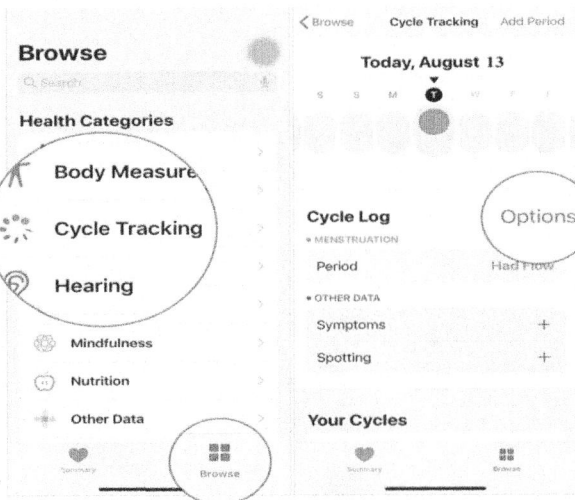

- Flip the Symptoms switch to ON and see the rundown of symptoms. Tap on the symptoms you're experiencing during your periods.

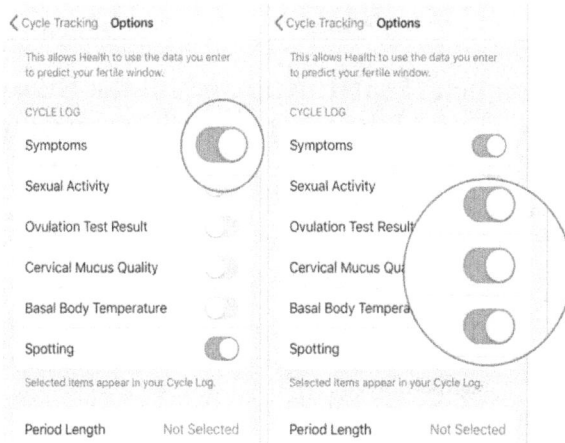

- Switch ON the **Ovulation Test Results** so as to see your logged ovulation test outcomes.
- Switch on options, for example, Cervical Mucus Quality, Basal Body Temperature, and Spotting to view the results.

This would give you a total idea with respect to your menstruation cycle and fertility, also if you want to give birth. Keep in mind these are simply predictions dependent on the information you enter in Cycle Tracking. It's constantly prescribed to consult a doctor before you decide on anything.

Receive Period Predictions and Notifications

- Launch **Health App** and hit the **Browse** tab to find the **Cycle Tracking** option.
- Tap on **Options,** which is directly beside **Cycle Log**.

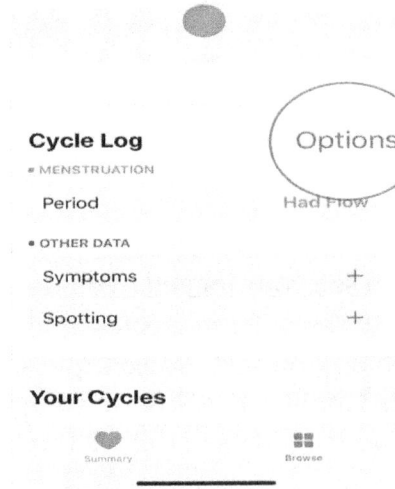

Cycle Log

● MENSTRUATION

Period

Options

Had Flow

● OTHER DATA

Symptoms   +

Spotting   +

Your Cycles

Summary   Browse

- Next, Toggle ON **Period Prediction** option to make a period prediction schedule for a two-month and Toggle ON **Period Notification** option to get updates to save your day by day information and get updates on your upcoming period.

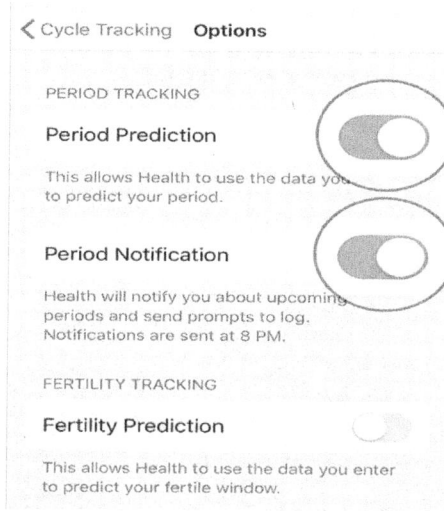

❮ Cycle Tracking **Options**

PERIOD TRACKING

Period Prediction

This allows Health to use the data you
to predict your period.

Period Notification

Health will notify you about upcoming
periods and send prompts to log.
Notifications are sent at 8 PM.

FERTILITY TRACKING

Fertility Prediction

This allows Health to use the data you enter
to predict your fertile window.

- The period prediction is one of the amazing highlights of Cycle Tracking in the Health app in iOS 13. Base on the first date of the period you entered, it'll establish a two-month schedule to predict in the next two months' your period time frame. This may be correct, yet sometimes it might go wrong too, as it's only a prediction all things considered.

Set Up Fertility Predictions and Notifications

- Launch the **Health App** and tap on the Browse tab
- Tap on the **Cycle Tracking** option.

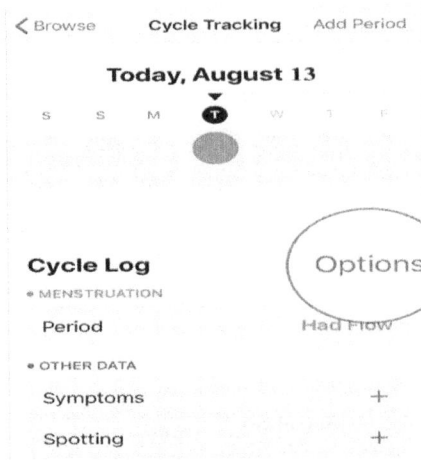

- Next, tap on **Options,** which is on the right side of **Cycle Log**.

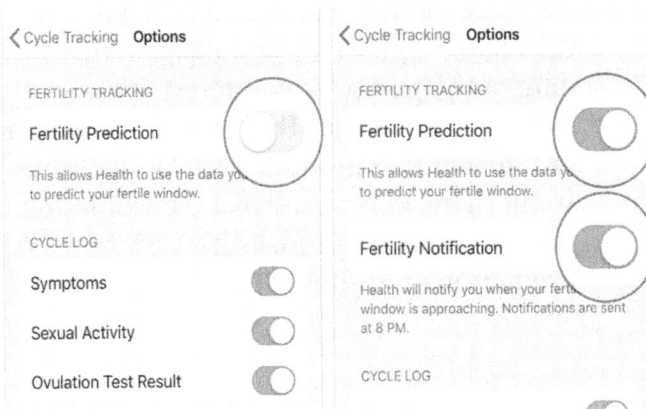

- In the fertility tracking segment, turn on **Fertility Prediction** and **Fertility Notification** to create a three-week schedule of next fertility and to get notifications about your next fertility window.

Manage Menstruation Flow

- Open **Health App**, go to the **Browse** tab, and tap on **Cycle Tracking** from the rundown.
- Tap on **Day** from the top and then tap on **Flow Level**.
- Note: Tap on **Add Period** from the top right corner if you have not logged your period date yet and select the date to begin.
- Next, select the flow level from the given options, for example, light, medium, heavy, unspecified (if you're not certain) or "**None**" and then tap on "**Done!**"
- Continue to do this until your period exists. This would help the app to be exact while predicting the period schedule and fertility frame. If you haven't included the previous month's period information, add it to get period calendar predictions now!

Add Cycle Symptoms to Cycle Tracking

- Open the **Health App** and then tap on the **Browse** tab
- Touch on the **Cycle Tracking** option.
- Tap on '+' icon next to Symptoms from other data section.

- Next, select the symptoms, for example, Headache, Lower Back Pain, and so forth, whichever you're encountering right now in the Cycle Tracking app. Tap on **"Done"** once you have selected these symptoms.

Remove Cycle Tracking Data

- Go to the **Cycle Tracking** option in the **Health App**.
- Tap on **View Cycle Tracking Items** from the bottom of the **Cycle Tracking** summary.
- Next, select the section or category log, for instance, **Cycle Tracking Symptoms**. After this, scroll down to bottom and tap on **Show All Data**.
- Tap on Edit at the upper right corner of the display
- Next, tap on **Remove Button** (red dot with a minus image inside)
- Finally, tap on **Delete** and afterward tap on **"Done."**

Disable True Tone Display

True Tone is a feature that automatically adjusts the white balance of your iPad's display to correct for changes in ambient light conditions.

- Open the **Settings** app on your iPad.
- Tap **Display & Brightness**.
- Toggle the True Tone switch to off.

Edit Videos on Your iPad

- In Photos, tap to open the video you want to edit or tap the Albums button at the bottom of your screen, scroll to the **Media Types** section, and choose **Videos**.
- Tap **Edit** in the top corner.
- A timeline bar at the foot of the screen displays every frame of your video. To edit the video, tap and hold either end of the timeline bar (look for the white bars at each end of the bar).
- Drag either end of the bar (which should now be yellow) to cut out the parts of the video you don't want to save. The part of the video displayed inside the yellow bar is what you'll save.

- In the app, you can only save continuous sections of the video. You can't cut out the beginning section and stitch together the end and middle of the video.
- When you're happy with your selection, tap "**Done**." If you change your mind and want to get rid of your selections, tap "**Cancel**."
- A menu will display with two options: "**Save as New Clip**" and "**Cancel**." Choose **Save as New Clip**. This saves the trimmed version of the video as a new file and leaves the original unscathed.
- The edited video will now be in your Photo albums as a separate video. You can now view and share it.

How to Record 4K Selfie

- Launch the **Settings** app on your iPad.
- Scroll down to find **Camera** and tap on it.
- Now, tap on **Record Video**.

- It's time to choose the desired resolution and frame rate.

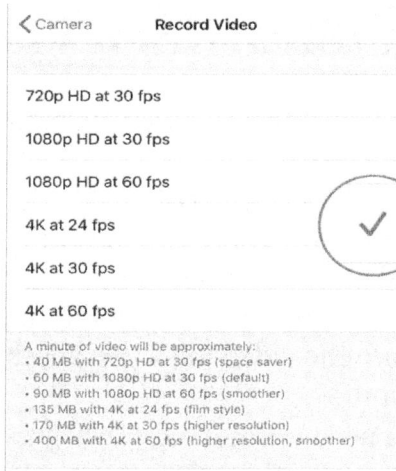

K at 24 fps: Choose it when you wish to shoot film style 4k video. Not to mention, it's also the most efficient option (from the storage management point of view) as it will take up just 135MB per minute.

4K at 30 fps: Go for this to record higher resolution selfie video. In terms of storage, it will take up 170MB per minute.

4K at 60 fps: Select it to shoot higher resolution and smoother selfie video. But keep it in mind, choose this storage hogging (400MB per minute) option only when you have a ton of storage on your device.

- Next, quit the **Settings** app and open the **Camera** app. Then, switch to the front camera and choose **Video**. After that, get ready to launch yourself and hit the red shutter button to start recording perfect selfies on your iPad 11 series.

Rotate/Straighten Videos

- Open the video in the **Photos app**.
- Tap on **Edit**.
- Tap on the **Crop icon**.
- You can now straighten the video if it was filmed at somewhat of an undulating angle. Simply swipe along the ruler beneath the video until you get the desired rotation.
- If you need to rotate it, 90-degrees (or more if essential!) tap on the rotate icon in the top left over the picture.
- When you're satisfied, tap "**Done.**" That's it!

Turn Off Attention Awareness Feature

- Go to **Settings**
- Tap on **Face ID & Passcode**
- Select **Attention Aware Features** and turn the feature off.

How to Enable/Disable Tap to Wake

- Go to **Settings**
- Touch **General**
- Tap **Accessibility**
- Next, touch **Tap to Wake**.
- Toggle on or off the feature base on preference.

Set Up Haptic Touch

Haptic Touch is Apple's name for touching and holding your finger on the screen.

- Go to **Settings**
- Select **Accessibility**

- Choose **Touch**
- Finally, tap **Haptic Touch**
- Choose **Fast** or **Slow**
- To test the feature, touch the flower or flashlight icon under the **Touch duration test**.

How to Use Sign In with Apple Feature

Sign in with Apple is the company's new sign-in option that will act as an alternative to creating custom log-ins for individual sites, or logging into them with Google or Twitter credentials. It's important for three reasons: The two-factor authentication makes it secure, it can save people from juggling complicated passwords, and Apple says it limits private data sharing with third parties.

- Open an app for the first time and click on the "**Sign in with Apple**" option, then confirm who you are with your device passcode or Face ID.

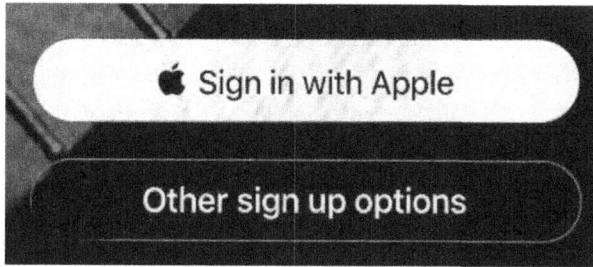

- There's no inventing another complicated password you'll have to remember or store in a password manager. You'll stay logged in on that device, and it works across other devices and on the Web. Developers can even add it to their Android apps.

- When you sign in with your Apple ID and select "**Private Email**," Apple creates a user-specific email address and forwards it to your original email address. You can share your email address only with trusted apps and websites.

CHAPTER SIX

Features of New Apple Maps App

Apple Maps is more detailed, more accurate, and has new options that can rival and even surpass Google Maps' equivalents.

Improved Details

Apple fitted hundreds of planes and cars with custom sensors and lidar and covered over 4 million miles to update the Maps app, resulting in more detailed and up-to-date maps. Buildings, roads, and other 3D structures are better represented in the app, and with more up-to-date maps, turn-by-turn directions are even better. These features are coming in a server-side update that Apple will trigger remotely.

Place Card Events

When you view information for a specific place on Maps, the interface for the place card screen is much easier to use and more helpful. Data is updated dynamically, including events at a location such as training sessions, movie theater times, and other activities, so the information displayed is most relevant to the current day.

Real-Time Transit Info

The new Maps app contains transit schedules for buses, subways, and trains, along with arrival times, stops in the line, and connections you can make. It also includes live updates for outages, cancellations, and other occurrences that will make your trip across town a hassle.

For example, in iOS 12, when you select something such as a train, then tap a stop, it just asks you to "**View on Map**," which would just show the full route of the train. Now, it clearly shows the stops in a list with upcoming departures shown as scheduled. Tapping "**View on Map**" in iOS 13 shows only the route from one station to your destination.

Faster Favorites Access

On the launch page, you can now add a button for the places you frequently travel to, such as home and work, which will appear in the "**Favorites**" section. Before, you'd have to scroll to the bottom of the launch page to see an option to view your favorites.

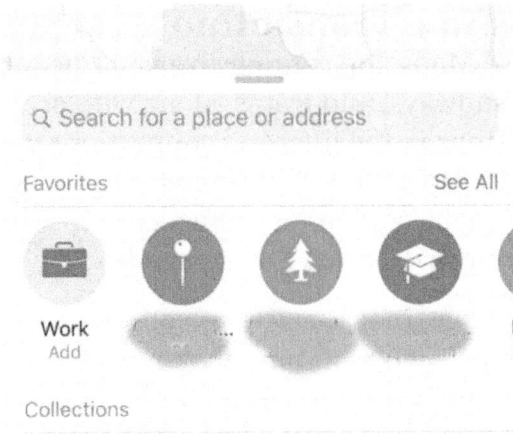

Based on your current location, a number, either in miles or minutes, will appear under a favorite's button to indicate your current distance from the place. Selecting any of the favorite locations will bring up the location details page, which not only shows you the fastest route to the site but lets you start navigation right away.

Reorganize Favorites
When viewing your list of favorites in iOS 12, what you see is what you get. But in iOS 13, you can move locations around in the list, so your most frequented places show up first on the launch page.

Collections
With iOS 13, you can keep your favorite places in your list of favorites and move everything else

into collections. That means less clutter and even faster access.

With collections, you can organize shops, restaurants, homes of loved ones, and more into folders, which you can share with friends, keep for later reference, or use to start navigation instantly. You can edit the lists easily and even upload a custom image the better fits the group of places.

Look Around

By far, one of the most significant features to finally make its way into Apple Maps is its very own version of Street View. Aptly named Look Around, the function can be accessed by zooming in on a target area and selecting the binoculars icon once it appears on the upper right just. Not all locations have "Look Around" views available.

Look Around gives you high-definition images of the exact location and provides a series of 3D images that you can scroll through as opposed to a simple 3D rendering. And if you want to continue to explore in this view, you can even select roads around you to "fast travel" the area, while retaining the same detailed images.

Look Around also lets you select labels to learn more information about the places around you, such as directions and ratings. It's also worth noting that besides the binoculars icon, you can also go into Look Around mode by selecting the feature on the app's information card when you

tap on a specific area, and it works in both
portrait and landscape.

Redesigned Feedback Tool

When Maps gives you a wrong turn or sends you
to the wrong place, it's not easy to send a report
to Apple to fix it for everyone else in the future.
But the Maps app in iOS 13 makes it easier with
an improved feedback form for submitting
incorrect addresses, business locations,
operating hours, categories, and more.

Flight Status Info

When you're traveling via air, Maps has you
covered. It now includes tons of information
pertaining to your flight, including terminal
locations, gate locations, departure times, and so
on.

Improved Voice Directions

When Siri gives you directions during
navigation, it can make things a little bit more
complicated to understand than necessary.
Something like "in 2,000 feet, turn left" doesn't
mean anything to someone who can't judge
distances like that, so Siri has changed to give a
more natural experience. With the better-
sounding Siri, that 2,000-feet line will end up
something like "turn left at the next traffic light."
Apple also states that Maps "guides you closer to

your end-point destination, which is especially important for large venues."

MapKit
While MapKit applies only to developers from an app-building perspective, iPad users will reap the benefits. Developers can utilize vector overlays for things like heat maps, weather, or buildings on top of the map, as well as filtering options for points of interest and camera zoom and pan limits. Also, it supports Dark Mode!

Better CarPlay Integration
If your vehicle has CarPlay, either factory-installed or aftermarket, the Maps app makes route planning easier, includes better search tools, and improves navigation. You can also view your Favorites and Collections with CarPlay.

Generate Lists of Locations Using Collections in Apple Map

Collections can come in handy when planning a trip. For instance, you can create a list of places to visit, then quickly view and get directions to them. Alternatively, if you have friends visiting and they ask for some must-see spots, you can create a collection and share it with them. Or if you just want to make a list of memorable places you've visited, collections will work for that, too.

#1: Make a New Collection

After opening the Maps app, you'll see a search bar and your list of favorites at the bottom of the screen. It'll be on the left side if you're in landscape orientation. Your list of collections is right below the favorites, so swipe up to view them.

When you do, you won't see any existing collections if its the first time using collections on the device. However, you may see some if you created them on another device that uses the same Apple ID. To make a new collection, tap the "**New Collection**" button, give the group a name, then tap the "**Create**" button in the upper right. Now you're ready to start filling your collection.

After you've created three or more collections, a "**See All**" button will appear in the upper right of the Collections section. You'll need to tap that, then tap the plus **(+)** button in the lower right to create new collections from then on.

#2: Add Locations to the Collection

There are a couple of different ways to add new locations to a collection. You can either add a place from within the collection itself or, if you are already viewing a site, you can choose which collection to add that location to.

Option 1: From the Collection Directly

Start by tapping the collection you'd like to add a location to. If there aren't any locations in the collection yet, a "+ **Add a Place**" button will be there. Otherwise, you can scroll up to reveal a toolbar at the bottom of the card, then tap the plus **(+)** button from there. (If you're in landscape view, the toolbar should already be shown.)

Tapping the button will open a search field that will let you search for locations, and it will also show you locations you've recently viewed. After performing your search, tap any of the places to add them to your collection.

Option 2: From the Location Itself

You can also add locations that you're currently viewing to your collections. After you've searched for a place, swipe up on the location's information card, and you'll see an "**Add to**" button underneath any user images available. Tap it, and then you can add it to an existing collection or create a new collection to add it to.

You can also add your current location to a collection. To do so, tap the location arrow icon in the upper right to center the map on your coordinates. Then, tap the blue dot on the map showing your location and select the "**Mark My Location**" button. Like locations you've searched for, the marked area will have an "Add to" button you can use to add your current location to a collection.

Use 'Look Around' to Navigate High-Resolution Street Views of Cities

When using Look Around to get a quick visual reference for ground-level details, you'll see that the imagery is high-resolution and interactive, so you can move seamlessly down a street or pan around to see 360-degree views of the area. Honestly,

- To see "**Look Around**" in action, open Apple Maps on your device and then browse the map or find a location using the search bar that supports the "Look Around" feature.
- When you browse to a location on the map via pinching, when you zoom in enough to clearly see some street names, a binoculars icon will appear in the top right. That's the "Look Around" icon. But it will only appear in supported locations.

- When you type in a location and select it from the list, you'll see the info card for the area open with buttons for "Flyover" and "Directions," as well as photos of the location. In the photos section, if it's a supported area, the first image will show a preview of the ground-level view with a "Look Around" button overlayed on it next to binoculars.

Viewing a Look Around Location

- Tap on the binoculars icon or "Look Around," and you'll be transported to a street view of the location, packed with the cars, buildings, homes, and blurry faces you're accustomed to on Google Maps.
- If you tap the binoculars icon on the map, the Look Around preview pane appears with the map still visible. That's useful if you're actually at the location and want to look around as you navigate streets. Otherwise, tapping the "Look Around" button in the info card will jump you right into full-screen mode for total immersion.
- When viewing the Look Around preview, you can tap the expand icon (the two arrows pointing away from each other) to enter full-screen mode. Likewise, when viewing the area in full-screen mode, you can tap the minimize icon (the two arrows pointing toward each other) to see the preview overtop the map.

Navigating a Look Around Location

We were hoping that as you move your tablet around, Look Around would automatically adjust the view, similar to what you can do using Flyover. Instead, it's touch-based navigation.

- Swipe left to move to the right, right to see to the left, down to view up, and up to view down.
- To move yourself to a different area in Look Around, tap the area you want to go to. It works similar to "Street View" in Google Maps, but much, much smoother. To get a closer look at a building or other object, pinch out with two fingers to zoom in. Pinching in with two fingers will zoom you back out to the default view.
- When viewing the minimized Look Around window, you can also drag the map around to change locations instantly. The binoculars always stay in the center, so the map moves, not the icon. Plus, you can tap a place on the map to jump there.
- Not every street will support Look Around in the area, but many roads that are lightly shaded blue with dark blue outlines will work. The binoculars show you the direction of what you're viewing and will spin around as you turn around in the Look Around window.

- In full-screen mode, a card at the bottom will display your location or approximate location as you move around the area. You can tap that to view options to share the location or report issues, as well as see when the imagery was taken.

Viewing Location Information in Look Around

When you're in the minimized view, there will be no overlayed information on the Look Around pane. But when you're in full-screen mode, you'll see street names, business names, and more. Better yet, you can tap on them to interact with them.

- Tapping a street name jumps you there. Similarly, tapping a business or location of interest marker will drop you there but also open an information card with reviews, photos, phone numbers, websites, and more. When not viewing a point of interest, you can tap the location card at the bottom to bring up the menu, which lets you "**Hide Labels**" for all streets and businesses, if you don't want to see them. Tap "**Show Labels**" to view them again.

Transit Directions, Ride-Sharing & Walking Directions

Maps can assist you in traversing by means of mass transit, ride-sharing service, and walking.

- Launch the Maps app and choose a destination.
- On the directions screen, tap **Transit**, **Ride** or **Walk**.
- Touch **Transit** to display selections using a bus, subway, light rail, ferry, etc. to get to your endpoint, if your local mass transit system has been mapped by Apple. Select your favored direction and tap "**Go.**"
- Touch **Ride** if you are in a region that supports ride-sharing. Your installed ride-sharing app, such as Uber and Lyft, opens, and its estimated price appears. Tap "**Next**" for the one you want to use.
- Touch **Walk** for a rundown of streets and roads to traverse by foot. Tap "**Go**" to start your walk.

If you want Maps to be set to default to one type of transportation, follow the steps below.

- Go to the **Settings** app
- Touch **Maps** and select either **Walking** or **Transit** in the **Preferred Transportation Type** section. That will do the trick!

Share Your Location Using the Apple Map

It's easy to share your location with friends and family directly from the Apple Map app via the steps below.

- Launch the Maps app on the Home screen.
- Tap the location arrow in the top right corner to ensure your location is precise.
- Touch the blue dot that denotes your current location.
- Next, click on **Share My Location**.
- In the sharing pane, choose how to share your location, either via Messages, Mail, and others.
- In the "**To**" text box, input the recipient or address details and then send the message.

CHAPTER SEVEN

How to Use Memoji Feature

- Open iMessage on your iPad and tap on create a new message icon.

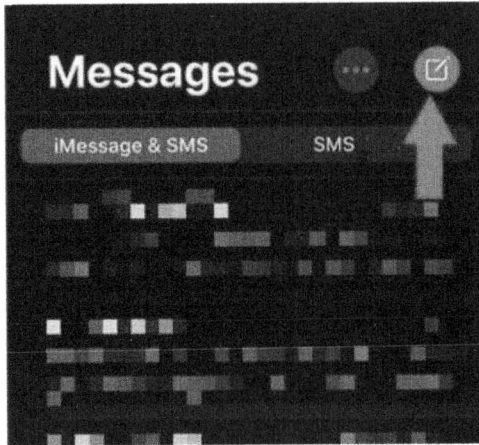

- Once it launches, you should see a new Memoji icon staring at you.

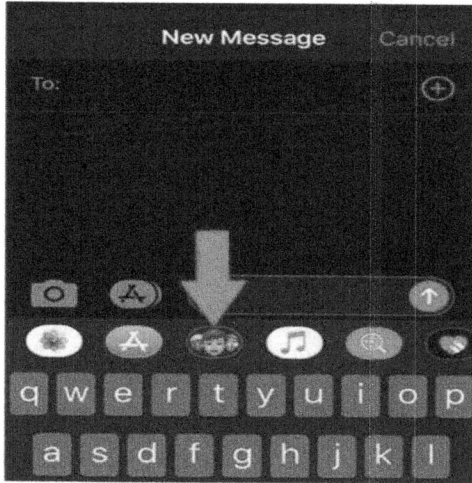

- Tap on it to launch Memoji, and you will be greeted with the "+" icon.

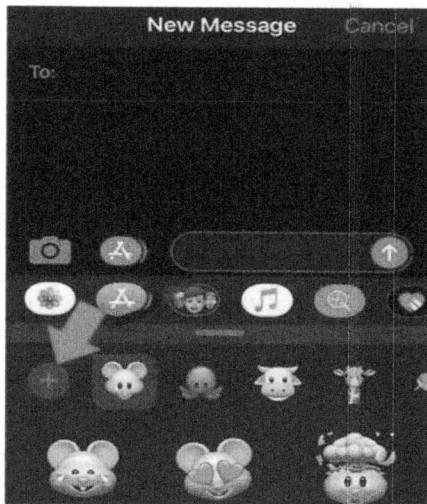

- Tap on that to begin creating your Memoji, which is nothing but your digital avatar. You will now begin customizing Memoji.

How to Create Memoji

- Choose from a variety of skin tones here. There is a slider to help you pan and select one. Select the freckles option.

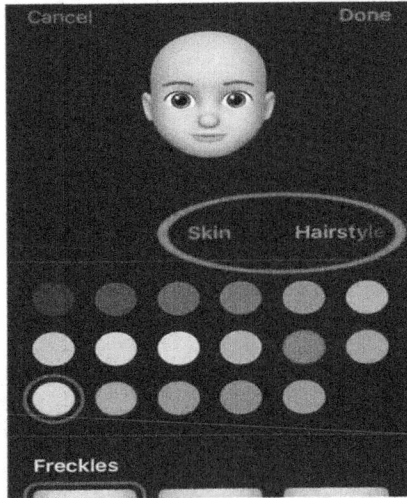

- Pick a hairstyle. To find hairstyles for men/boys, scroll a little more. Apple has decided not to go the gender way, so everything is available on the same screen. Continue with choosing your head and nose shape. Then select appropriate eyebrows for your Memoji.
- You can also cycle between appropriate nose shape, and also pick ear piercings if you have any or just want to use them on the Memoji. Finally, there are eye and headwear options to complete the look.

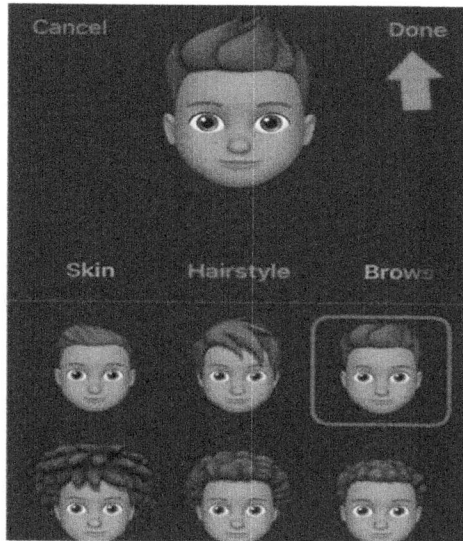

- Tap on "**Done**" to save. Do not go back at any point during the process because you will have to begin from scratch. That said, it doesn't take more than a few moments either. After you make your Memoji, iOS 13 will create a bunch of stickers automatically.

Edit, Delete or Create Another Memoji

- Go back to iMessages and either start a new conversation or enter an existing one. Instead of the "+" icon, you will see a menu icon. Tap on it to find some new options.

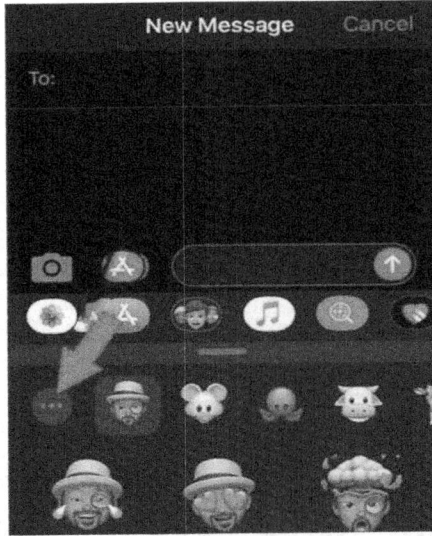

- Tap on the **New Memoji** button to begin the process all over again.

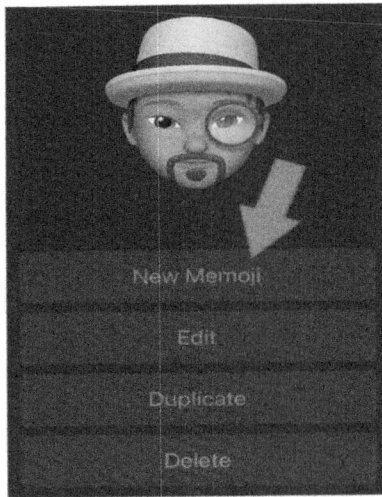

- Tap on the **Edit** button to change features of the current or selected Memoji. Finally, tap on the **Delete** option to delete the Memoji.

- Tap on the **Duplicate** button to create the exact same Memoji, and then quickly change certain features to create a new one on the fly.
- Every new Memoji you create will be in the gallery with its respective set of stickers. Pretty fun.

How to Remove Memoji Option

- Open a new message or reply to an old one, and tap on **More**.

- You will then select **Edit**.

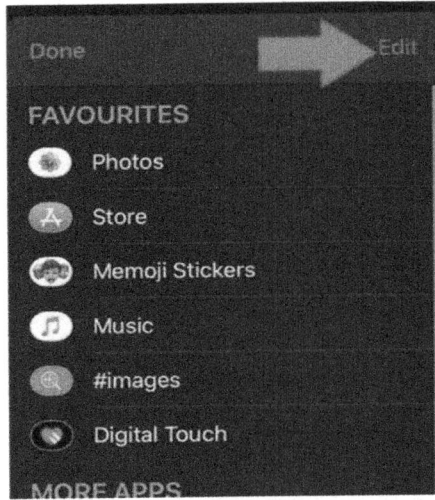

- Tap on the "-" icon next to the Memoji button to remove it from the list.
- You can add and remove other features similarly.

How to Use Siri Shortcuts

Siri Shortcuts allows you to do regular tasks rapidly, and with the apps, you utilize the most with only a tap or by asking Siri. Siri learns your routines across your apps. Siri then recommends a simple method to perform common tasks on the Lock screen or in Search. For instance, if you request news flash consistently on an app, Siri may recommend your preferred news.

- To utilize a Siri Suggestion, simply tap it on the lock screen. On the other hand, swipe down from the center of your screen to show **Search**; at that point, tap the **Siri Suggestion**.

Add Shortcuts to Siri

You can likewise run any shortcut by asking Siri. Search for the "**Add to Siri**" button in your most-used apps and tap to include with your very own expression or then again go to **Settings** to find all shortcuts accessible on your iPad.

Shortcuts that require an app to open on your iPad won't take a shot at HomePod and Apple Watch.

Add Shortcut from a third-party App

- Launch the third-party app and tap **Add to Siri**.

- Tap (red icon). At that point, record a personal catchphrase that you'll say to Siri to run the shortcut. Ensure that you record an easy expression that you'll recall.

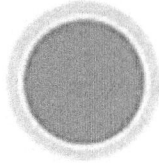

- Tap "**Done.**"

Add Shortcut from Settings

- Go to **Settings > Siri & Search**.
- You'll see three proposed shortcuts. Tap **All Shortcuts** to see more actions from various apps.
- Tap **Plus**.

- To record a personal expression, tap (red icon). Attempt to record an easy expression that you'll recall.
- Tap "**Done.**"

Delete a shortcut or change the phrase

- Head to **Settings > Siri & Search** and touch My Shortcuts.

- To change the expression for the shortcut, tap the shortcut, at that point, tap **Re-Record Phrase**.
- To erase a shortcut, swipe left over the shortcut and then tap **Delete**. Alternatively, tap the shortcut and tap **Delete Shortcut**.

How to Set Screen Time

- Tap the "**Settings**" app.
- Select "**Screen Time**."
- Tap "**Turn on screen time**."
- Touch "**Continue**."
- Tap "**This is an iPad for children**."
- Tap "**Done**"
- Next, tap "**Done**."
- Tap "**Continue**."
- Enter the passcode.
- Input the passcode again.

Restrict Functions of Apps

You can restrict the use of various apps by following the settings below.

- Launch the "**Settings**" app.
- Tap "**Screen Time**."
- Touch "**Content & Privacy Restrictions**."

- Enter the screen time passcode.
- Tap "**Allowed App**."
- Turn off apps you want to restrict.
- When you check the home screen, the app icon disappears, and usage is restricted.

Restrict Use of Contents
- Tap the "**Settings**" app.
- Tap "**Screen Time**."
- Tap "**Content & Privacy Restrictions**".
- Enter the screen time passcode.
- Tap "**Content Restriction**."
- Tap "**App**."
- Set the App rate that is allowed to use, and the setting is complete.

Restrict Access to Websites
- Tap the "**Settings**" app.
- Tap "**Screen Time**."
- Tap "**Content & Privacy Restrictions**".
- Enter the screen time passcode.
- Tap "**Content Restriction**."
- Tap "**Web Content**."
- Select one of the following settings depending on the intensity you want to limit.
- Tap "**Restrict adult website**."
- Tap "**Only allowed websites**."

- Always tap the "**Add Web Site**" permission.
- Enter the URL and tap, "**Done.**"
- Allowed websites are added to "**Always Allowed.**"

Change Screen Brightness

- Go to the **Settings** app
- Choose "**Screen Display & Brightness**"
- Adjust the brightness by moving the slider displayed in "**Brightness**" left or right

Turn on Automatic Brightness Adjustment

- Launch the **Settings** app on your iPad
- Go to "**Accessibility**"
- Select "**Screen Display & Text Size**"
- Turn "**automatic brightness adjustment**" on/off.

Shorten Automatic Lock

- Launch the **Settings** app on your iPad
- Go to "**Screen Display & Brightness**"
- Select "**Auto Lock**"

- Set the time until automatic lock. The display does not go dark while looking at the screen.

CHAPTER EIGHT

How to Change wallpaper

- Launch the **Settings** app on your iPad
- Go to "**Wallpaper**"
- Select "**Select wallpaper.**"
- Select the photo or image you want to set as wallpaper
- At the lower right of the device, tap "**Settings.**"
- Tap **Set to locked screen / Set to home screen / Set for both**.

Turn On One-Handed Mode

The iPad 11 series are longer, making it difficult for your fingers to reach the buttons and icons displayed at the top of the screen.

- Launch the **Settings** app on your iPad
- Go to "**Accessibility**"
- Select "**Touch**"
- Switch on "**Easy Access**"

Add Widget to Display the Battery Level as a Percentage

- Pair with a Bluetooth device such as AirPods, Apple Watch, or wireless earphone
- On the first page of your device home screen, slide left to access **"Today's View."**
- Tap "**Edit**"
- Tap "**+**" next to "**Battery**" to add a battery widget.

How to Take Smarter Selfies

- Base on default settings, if you hold your iPad 11 vertically, the image sensor will zoom in to take a 7-megapixel selfie. For a full 12-megapixel shoot, touch the expand button on the screen to zoom out for a smarter selfie.
- Rotate your device for a horizontal selfie, though, the camera will automatically zoom out for 12-megapixel selfies. Alternatively, you can also zoom back in

for a 7-megapixel shot if you prefer that
instead.

How to Control Offload
Unused Apps

Remove unused apps on your device to free up
storage space. In addition to automatically
removing apps when the remaining storage
capacity is low, you can also remove any apps
manually.

- By selecting "**iTunes Store & App
  Store**" from "**Settings**" on your iPad and
  turning on "**Offload Unused Apps**,"
  apps that are not in use are automatically
  used when the iPad storage capacity is low
  will be removed.

Restrict Offload Unused
Apps

- From the **Settings** app, tap **Screen
  Time**.
- Next, tap to turn on **Content & Privacy
  Restrictions**.
- Then, directly underneath, tap **iTunes &
  App Store Purchases**.

- Tap **Deleting Apps**.
- Follow the arrow to the next screen and touch **Don't Allow**.
- With that control set, no one can delete apps from your device from now on unless you explicitly lift the restriction.

Move Home Screen Apps

- First, press and hold any icon.
- Then, a thumbprint will be displayed on the upper left of the icon, as shown in the image below, and it will move like a wave.
- The icon can now be moved.
- Then press the icon you want to move with your finger.
- Move your finger to the place you want to move without releasing your finger.
- By the way, you can't place app icons anywhere on your iPad or iPad, like Android smartphones.
- There may be cases where you can use unofficial app icons, but basically, app icons are arranged in order from the top.

Moving Apps to Another Page
Next, I will explain how to move to another page when moving the icon.

- Long press the app

- A thumbprint appears on all icons
- Keep pressing the icon you want to move with your finger
- Move to the page you want to move
- Switch to the page you want to move and place an icon.

Create a Folder on the Home Screen

- First, press and hold the icon.
- To delete, move, or create a folder, you must first press and hold the icon, the thumbprint is displayed, and the icon is wavy.
- You can now edit the home screen icons.
- First, tap the icons you want to organize into a folder.
- Move the icons in the previous chapter so that they overlap the icons you want to put together in the same folder.
- Then, a folder is automatically created.
- Move and place the icon in the folder as it is.

Reset Icon Layout on Home Screen

- Go to **Settings** app
- Tap **General**
- Tap **Reset Home Screen Layout.**

Enable Location Services on Find My App

To use the Find My app, you have to enable location services on your iPad. The flows below will guide you on that.

- Go to **Settings**
- Tap **Privacy**.
- Select **Location Services**.
- Toggle on **Location Services**.
- If you would like to share your location with others, you can do that from this area of the Settings as well by tapping **Share My Location** and turning on the toggle on the next screen.

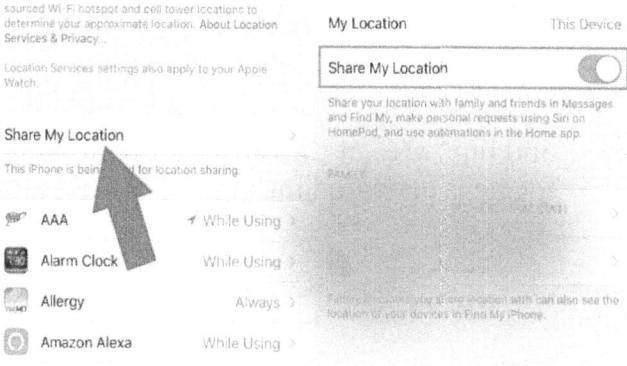

sourced Wi-Fi hotspot and cell tower locations to determine your approximate location. About Location Services & Privacy...

Location Services settings also apply to your Apple Watch.

Share My Location   >

This iPhone is being used for location sharing.

🚗 AAA   ◂ While Using >

🕰 Alarm Clock   While Using >

💊 Allergy   Always >

🔵 Amazon Alexa   While Using >

My Location   This Device

Share My Location   ⬤

Share your location with family and friends in Messages and Find My, make personal requests using Siri on HomePod, and use automations in the Home app.

Turning on sharing your iPhone location with can also see the location of your devices in Find My iPhone.

Another way to do this is demonstrated below;

- Go to **Settings**
- Touch your **Apple ID** at the top
- Click on "**Find My**"
- Next, turn on **Share My Location**.

Locate Family/Friends on Find My App

If you need to locate someone who has shared their location with you, it's easy and simple.

- Launch "Find My" app
- Touch People at the bottom and touch the person on your list. You'll then view their location on the map.
- You also have preferences to Contact them, get Directions to their spot, add Notifications, and lots of other kinds of stuff.

Share Your Location via Find My App

- To share your location, launch Find My and tap "**Me**" at the bottom. Ensure the toggle is activated for Share My Location.

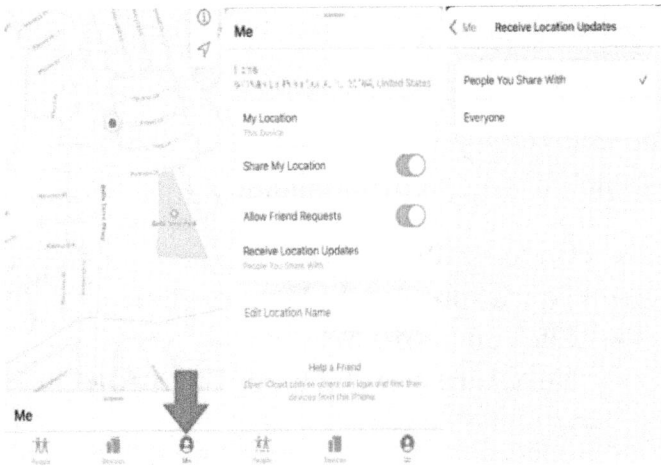

- You have a preference also to **Allow Friend Requests**, choose to **Receive Location Updates** with everyone or only people you share with, and **Edit Location Name**.

Enable Offline Finding via Find My App

- Launch the "Find My" app and choose **Devices** at the bottom. You'll see each of your devices on the list at the bottom, along with their locations on the map.

- Tap to select a particular device and then **Play Sound** to help you find it or get **Directions** to it. You can also "**Mark As Lost**" and get **Notifications** when the device is found. If you deem it fit, you can remotely **Erase This Device**.

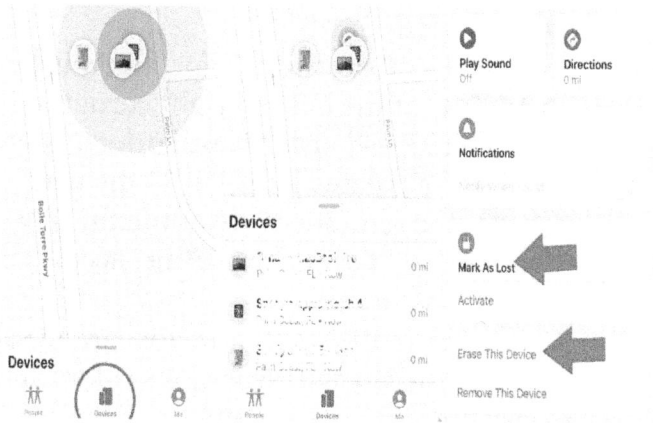

- You can also use this feature to find iOS devices belonging to others who've shared their location with you. For instance, if your friend lost their device, their devices will show up in the list for you to choose and locate the same way you locate yours.

Verify Offline Finding is Turned On

- Open the **Settings** app and tap your name up top to view your Apple ID settings.
- Touch "**Find My**" option.
- Next, tap "**Find My iPad**."
- On the page that pops up, make sure "**Enable Offline Finding**" is turned on.

How to Create a New Reminder

- Launch the "**Reminder**" app and touch "**Add list**" at the bottom right corner of the screen. Previously "**Reminders**" were just a list of created lists, but in the new version, the reminders are automatically organized to "**Today**" or "**Flag**" according to the set contents.
- Next, register the name and appearance of the list. You can choose various colors and icons according to the content. After setting, tap "**Done**" at the top right of the screen. The newly created list will be added to "**My List**," so select it.
- Tap "**New Reminder**" at the bottom left of the screen and enter the name of the reminder. At this time, you can set the date and time to receive notifications by tapping the icon displayed on the keyboard. You can also add flags, photos, and scanned documents.

Receive Notification When Sending Message via Reminder App

- To set it, first tap the "**i**" icon displayed at the right end of the reminder, then tap "**Notify when sending a message**."
- Next, select the contact of the other party. Send a message to the person you choose here to receive a reminder notification.
- Try sending a message to the person you selected. If you forget the event and send a casual message, you will receive a reminder reminding you of the event.

Remove Reminder

- The first is to select only the items you want to delete and delete them manually. Open the list and swipe left on the reminder you want to erase. When "**Delete**" appears, swipe further to the left. Only one event has been deleted.
- The second method is to delete the list itself. Open the list and tap "**Delete List**" at the top right of the screen. Tap "**Delete**" again to delete the list itself. Use it when you have achieved all of your goals.

Creating Grouped Lists via Reminder App

- First, you can tap "**Edit**" in the top right, then "**Add Group**" in the bottom left.

That will prompt the **New Group** modal to open, but before we get to that, let's go over the second way to initiate a new grouping.

- Second, press-and-hold on one of your lists to catch it, drag it above another list that you want it grouped with, then drop it when the bottom list is highlighted. The **New Group** modal should open.

- You can only create grouped lists in iCloud, not third-party services. So if you have a Yahoo or Outlook section with lists in it you want to consolidate, it will have to wait until those services support it. Additionally, you cannot drag one list from one service over to a list that's in iCloud; lists stay put in their own accounts.

- Either way, in the **New Group** modal, choose a name for your lists group. After, you can view the lists that are included in the group via the "**Include**" menu item. There, you can remove some of the lists from the group (hit the red minus button) or other lists you already have (the green plus).

- If you want to change the order of your included lists, hold down on the three-bar icon on the right of a list and drag it up or down to where you want it. When you're all set, tap "**Create**" to finish.

Add New Subtasks to Reminder

- So either create a "**New Reminder**" to be the parent or tap on a reminder in the list already that you want to be the parent. Next, tap on its information (*i*) icon to open its **Details** modal view. Tap on "**Subtasks**" near the bottom, then "**Add Reminder**" for each subtask you want to create.

- To make sure newly added subtasks are saved, hit the "**return**" or "**enter**" key on the keyboard or hit "**Add Reminder**" again after typing one out. That will pop you into a new bubble for the next subtask to add.

- If you add a subtask you didn't want, edit it to something else or short-swipe left on it and hit "**Delete**," or long-swipe left to remove it automatically. When no more subtasks are needed, tap "**Details**" to go back. While you can't flag all of the subtasks from the main Details page, you can toggle on "**Flagged**" to flag the parent. Doing so won't flag all the subtasks underneath, only the parent. Toggle it back off to unflag it. Hit "**Done**" to finalize things.

Tag a Contact in the Reminder App

- Tap on your selected or new reminder to bring up the information button, then tap that (*i*) to bring up the Details settings, where you can add notes and configure a handful of parameters.

- Select the toggle for "**Remind me when messaging,**" so it's on, tap the new "**Choose Person**" option, then pick a contact from the list that pops up, either by browsing or searching.
- After doing so, you'll return to the reminder's settings with your contact tagged under the toggle.
- If you want to choose another person, tap "**Edit**," then tap another contact from the list. When satisfied with your selection, tap "**Done**." You'll see your chosen contact tagged on the reminder in any list view of the app itself, a helpful way to quickly identify which reminders have messaging tags.

CHAPTER NINE

Enable/Disable Swipe Typing

- Launch the **Settings**
- Select **General**.
- Scroll down and tap **Keyboard**.
- Next, scroll down to Slide to Type and disable it. If you need to enable it, you can basically enable it once more.
- If you need the delete key to remove one letter rather than the entire word, go to **Delete Slide-to-Type by Word** and disable it.

How to Use Swipe Type

Swipe-typing is enabled by default. All you have to do to get swiping is simply start swiping.

- Spot a finger on your screen and drag it over the letters of the word you need to type. Let's say you want to type "mind," you would tap on the "m" key, and drag your finger over the "i," "n," and "d" letters in successive order. The keyboard will, at that point, foresee the word you're typing.

- The advantage of swipe-typing is that it's generally a lot quicker than tapping on each key in progression. After swiping, the keyboard will present three options for your swiped word, so you can tap to choose the one you need. However, if the middle prediction is right, start swiping your next word to auto-select it.
- Those predictions will get progressively accurate the more you utilize your keyboard. However, you can swap between tapping and swiping whenever, and there's no need to adjust any settings to change.

Set a Custom Name and Profile Picture via iMessage

- Open iMessage/Message App from the Home Screen.
- Tap on **Ellipsis (...)** located in the upper right corner of the screen.
- Tap on the **Edit Name** and **Photo** tab.
- Next, tap on **Edit** from the Profile photo
- You can choose between Apple Suggestions for Profile photo or the Animoji available.
- If you want to use the Suggestions option, you can set Profile photo by snapping a

photo right direct from the camera app, or you may choose from your photo gallery.

To set Profile Picture using a captured image:

- Tap on the Camera icon from the Suggestion option.
- Capture an image.
- Once the image of choice is captured, move, and scale the captured image from the camera, make sure correctly crop the image to fit in the circular frame of the Profile Photo.
- Tap on **Use Photo**
- Select your filter of choice to change the appearance of the captured image.
- Tap "**Done**" to apply changes.

If you want to use the photos from your photo gallery on your device:

- Tap on the **All Photo** option and select the desired photo from photo albums
- Once the desired photo is selected, move and scale the photo to adjust its size making sure it fits in the circular frame, then
- Tap on **Choose**.
- Make necessary changes in appearance if desired by selecting the available filters.
- Tap "**Done**" to apply changes.

If you want to choose Animoji or personal Memoji:

- Select the Animoji or Memoji of your choice from the Animoji and Memoji from the choices available .You can also select a pose for the Animoji.
- Tap on **Next**.
- Move and Scale the selected Animoji or Memoji.
- Tap on **Choose**
- Select a Color for your Animoji Background
- Tap "**Done**" to apply changes.
- After every change made with the Profile Picture, you will notice a prompt "if you want to use this image in all places? Your ID and My Card in Contacts will be updated with this image" You can tap on either of the options "**Not now**" & "**Use**."
- Tap "**Done**" again. You will now see your desired Profile Photo.

Share Custom Name and Profile Photo

Having a Profile Picture and Profile Name on your iMessage Profile in iOS 13 does not necessarily mean that it will now be available for others to view or to be displayed. For privacy and security purpose, you still have the option of whether or not share your iMessage Profile. For additional information, there are two methods on how to share the iMessage profile:

Method 1:

- Open the iMessage/Message app
- Tap on Ellipsis (...) located in the upper right corner of the screen
- Tap on **Edit Name** and Photo option
- Toggle on the **Name and Photo Sharing** option
- Choose to **Share Automatically to Contacts Only** (Profile Name and Profile Picture will be shared automatically) or **Always ask** option (a prompt will appear if you want to share your iMessage Profile to a particular person).
- Tap "**Done**" to apply new changes.

Method 2:

- Go to **Settings** from the Home Screen
- Scroll down from the list of apps, and tap on **Messages**.
- Look for the **Share Name and Photo** option, then tap on it.
- Choose to **Share Automatically for Contacts Only** (Profile Name and Profile Picture will be shared automatically to your contacts) or **Always ask** option (a prompt appears every time to ask if you want to share your iMessage Profile to a particular person).
- Tap "**Done**" to apply new changes.

Delete your iMessage Profile Image

- Go to the **Settings** app.
- Select **Messages** from the rundown.
- Choose the option tagged **Share Name & Photo**.
- Touch **Edit** below your current iMessage profile picture.
- On the following screen, touch **Edit**.
- Next, tap **Delete**, then select **Delete** from the popup menu to confirm the action.
- Tap "**Done**" to save the changes made.
- Your iMessage profile image will now appear blank.

Pair a DualShock 4 Controller with Your iPad

- Go to your iPad Settings and ensure that Bluetooth is on
- Grab your PS4 DualShock 4 controller
- Push and hold the PS button and share button at the same time for 5 seconds
- After 5 seconds you should see the lightbar start to blink
- Go back to your iPad, and under Bluetooth, you should see "**DualShock 4 Wireless Controller**" listed

- Tap on it to connect
- Your PS4 DualShock 4 controller's light bar will turn pink once it has been successfully connected

Pair Xbox One Controller With iPad

- Go to your iPad Settings and ensure that Bluetooth is on
- Grab your Xbox One controller
- Press and hold the wireless button on your Xbox One controller for a few seconds (the button is located at the top of the controller towards the back)
- The light on the Xbox button will begin to blink
- Go back to your iPad, and under Bluetooth, you should see "**Xbox Wireless Controller.**"
- Tap on it to connect.
- If it has been successfully connected, the Xbox button's light will stop flashing and will remain lit.

Unpair DualShock 4/Xbox One S controller

- Launch **Settings** on your iPad.
- Tap on **Bluetooth**.
- Locate your DualShock 4 or Xbox controller in the device list, and then touch the "*i*" button.
- Choose to **Forget this device**.
- Confirm the unpairing by tapping on **OK**.

How to Use the New Text Format Gesture

Apple introduced a series of new gestures designed to make copying, pasting, and general text gestures easier and more intuitive, as well as undo on iOS 13.

In addition, new cursor navigation gestures, improved text selection, and intelligent text selection are much easier to implement and are a nice present for iPad users.

How to Copy
- Once you've highlighted the text, pinch with three fingers. It's easiest to complete

a three-finger gesture using "thumb, forefinger, and middle finger" or "thumb, thumb, forefinger, and ring finger." You have to be careful, the fourth finger touches the display, and it returns to the home screen

- If you perform the gesture correctly, you will see a small "copy" bubble at the top of the screen.

How to Cut

- Once you highlight the text, pinch twice with three fingers to "thumb, forefinger, and middle finger" or, to complete a three-finger gesture by using the "thumb, thumb, index finger, and ring finger" the most it's simple
- If you perform the gesture correctly, you will see a small "cut" bubble at the top of the screen.

How to Paste

- With the text copied, move to where you want to paste, pinch out with the same three fingers as when copying.
- If you perform the gesture correctly, you will see a small "paste" bubble at the top of the screen.

How to Cancel
Swipe left with three fingers

How to Start over
Swipe right with three fingers

How to Undo/Redo
- With three-finger swipe to the left or double-tap with three fingers only, you can undo the last operation, redo the last action, swipe to the right with three fingers.

Improved Intelligent Text Selection
- Place your finger on the first word and wait until it is highlighted (approximately 0.5 seconds)
- When the highlight is confirmed, drag to the end of where you want to select and release.

Select Entire Sentence or Text Paragraph
- Quickly highlight using a tap like macOS. Double-tap to select individual words, triple tap to select sentence, quadruple tap to select an entire paragraph.

With these improvements, working with a software keyboard will save you a lot of time.

How to Customize Zoom Function

- Use the three fingers to use the zoom function. Double-click on the screen with three fingers to zoom in, and double-tap again with three fingers to return to the original magnification. Double-tap with three fingers and drag to change the magnification, and you can enlarge up to 15 times. Because it is a considerably large magnification, you can check even more detailed parts.
- When moving in the zoom window, drag with three fingers. You can also change the display in the zoom window from " **Settings app > Accessibility> Zoom**." Invert, grayscale, grayscale inversion, low illumination, and display modes can be customized as required.
- If it is difficult to view small details such as text and images, use this zoom function to check while zooming in.

How to Customize VoiceOver

VoiceOver is a function that reads out the screen so that even people with visual impairments can use the iPad. The selected screen display will be read by the iPad on behalf of the user.

You can also change the speed and pitch at which the screen display is read out using VoiceOver. Detailed settings can be changed in "**Settings app** > **Accessibility** > **VoiceOver**.

How to Tap and Drag the Volume Indicator

When you adjust the volume, a volume adjustment bar is displayed in front of the screen in the middle of the screen. In iOS 13, this surprisingly disturbing screen has been improved and moved to the left of the volume button. It doesn't get in the way of the screen, it's great!

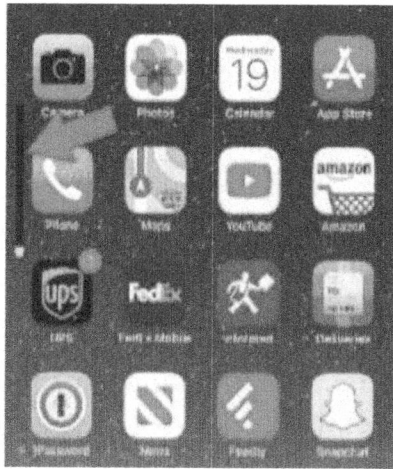

- By the way, if you press the volume control lever twice or more, the size will be reduced further. This bar can also be adjusted by sliding it directly on the screen, so it's a good idea to remember!
- Note that if "**Change by button**" is enabled in the "**Settings**" app, the volume is displayed at the top of the screen and cannot be touched.

How to Set Up CarPlay

- If your car is compatible with CarPlay, you can activate and operate Siri by long-pressing the voice control button.
- In that case, you can operate without tapping the monitor screen, so you can use iPad apps more safely while driving.

123

- To start using CarPlay, you need to connect your iPad and car.

There are two ways to do this: connecting a cable to the USB port and pairing via Bluetooth.

- To connect by wire, simply connect to a USB port that supports CarPlay with the iPad's Lightning-USB cable, but if you want to connect wirelessly, you need to do it from the settings app to pair with Bluetooth.
- Go to the "**Settings app.**"
- Tap "**General.**"
- Touch "**CarPlay > Available cars**" and then choose your car.

CHAPTER TEN

How to Use Sidecar

In 2019 the Apple introduced the Sidecar MacOS Catalina and iPadOS 13. The feature lets you use your iPad to mirror or extend the display of the Mac, as if a second screen.

What are the requirements for using Sidecar?

MacOS Catalina (10.15) version and MacOS iPad 13, both released in 2019, are required on Mac.

Other requirements include:

The Mac must not be sharing its internet connection.

Mac and iPad must be within 10 meters of each other.

Bluetooth, Wi-Fi, and Handoff features are all turned on.

The iPad must not be sharing its cellular connection.

Here's a list of supported Mac devices.

- iMac 27-inch (late 2015 or newer)
- MacPro (2016 or newer)
- Mac mini (2018)
- Mac Pro (2019)

- MacBook Air (2018)
- MacBook (early 2016 or newer)

To use the Sidecar feature on your iPad, your tablet must support the first or second-generation Apple Pencil. These include:

Apple Pencil:

- iPad Air (3rd generation
- iPad mini (5th generation)
- iPad (7th generation)
- iPad (6th generation)
- iPad Pro 12.9-inch (2nd generation)
- iPad Pro 12.9-inch (1st generation)
- iPad Pro 10.5-inch
- iPad Pro 9.7-inch
- Apple Pencil (2nd generation):
- iPad Pro 12.9-inch (3rd generation)
- iPad Pro 11-inch

How to Use iPad as a Second Screen
Click the AirPlay icon in the menu bar and select to connect with iPad

The iPad will now display an extension of the Mac screen;

If you want to mirror the screen, click again on the AirPlay menu (now a blue Sidecar rectangle) and select the option to mirror the screen.

Another way to access Sidecar is through System Preferences:

- Click on the Apple icon in the top left corner of your Mac
- Select System Preferences
- Click on Sidecar.

From this screen, you can connect and disconnect iPad from Sidecar, set the sidebar position, display or not the Touch Bar (even on Macs that do not have the component), and double-click the Apple Pencil.

The user can use iPad with Sidecar without connecting any wires, as long as they are at least 10 meters away. Using the iPad connected to your Mac will charge it while it is used as a second screen.

When Sidecar is on, a feature icon will appear on the iPad home screen to allow Apple tablet applications to be used normally. When switching to an iPad app, the Sidecar session is suspended; to reconnect it, simply return to the feature app.

How to Move Windows from Mac to iPad with Sidecar

There are two ways to move windows from Mac to iPad: just drag the window to the tablet or hover over the green button in the upper left corner of the window and tap the "Move to iPad" option.

How to Use Apple Pencil on Your iPad

Link the Apple Pencil with the iPad

You can use the Apple Pencil with the iPad Pro and other compatible iPad devices. The first time you use the Apple Pencil, remove the cover and connect it to the iPad Lightning connector.

When the Link button appears, press it.

Once you have linked the Apple Pencil, it will remain that way until you restart the iPad, activate Airplane mode, or link it to another iPad. You only have to link the Apple Pencil again when you want to use it.

Draw and Sketch with Apple Pencil

You can use the Apple Pencil to write, highlight, and draw with the integrated apps and other apps from the App Store. With some apps, such as Notes, you can draw and make sketches with an Apple Pencil.

To draw or make sketches in the Notes app:

- Open Notes

- Press .

- To draw, press . If you don't see , you should update your notes. To make sketches, press and then **Add** drawing.

- Start drawing or sketching. You can choose between several colors and drawing tools, and switch to the eraser if you make a mistake. When you draw or make sketches, you can tilt the Apple Pencil to shade the lines and press more to make them darker.

- If you draw near the edge of the screen with the Apple Pencil, iPadOS will not activate the Control Center, the Notification Center, or Multitasking. You can draw anywhere on the screen without being interrupted.

Charging the Apple Pencil

You can charge the Apple Pencil by plugging it into the iPad Lightning connector. You can also charge it with a USB power adapter if you use the charger adapter that included the Apple Pencil. The Apple Pencil will charge quickly when plugged into either of these two power supplies.

To see how much battery the Apple Pencil has left, check the widget view on the iPad.

Charge Tips

- You can replace the tip of the Apple Pencil if it is worn or damaged. The box contains a spare tip, and you can buy more if necessary. Simply unscrew the one you have and screw the new one.
- If the Apple Pencil does not link to the iPad
- Restart the iPad and try to link it again.
- Go to **Settings> Bluetooth** and check that this option is enabled.
- On the same screen, look for your Apple Pencil on **My devices** if you find it, press (i). Then press **Skip device**.
- Connect the Apple Pencil to the iPad and press the Link button when it appears after a few seconds.
- If it does not appear, wait a minute while the Apple Pencil charges. Then disconnect it, reconnect it and wait until the Link button appears.
- If it still does not appear, contact Apple Technical Support.

Apple Pencil Compatibility

The first-generation Apple Pencil works with the following iOS devices:

- iPad Air (3rd generation)
- iPad mini (5th generation)
- iPad (6th and 7th generations)
- iPad Pro 12.9 inch (1st and 2nd generations)
- iPad Pro 10.5 inch
- iPad Pro 9.7 inch

The second-generation Apple Pencil works with:

- iPad Pro 12.9 inch (3rd generation)
- iPad Pro 11-inch

Zip and unzip files on your iPad

Zipping and unzipping of files is now easy with the iPadOS and requires no third party app.

Zip Files on iPad

You can easily compress files by using the Files app on your iPad.

- Launch the Files app and go to the folder containing the files you want to zip.
- Click on **Select** on the top right.

- Mark the files you'd like to zip.
- Tap **More** on the bottom right and tap **Compress**.
- An Archive.zip file will display within that same folder and contain the files you zipped.

Unzip Files on iPad

You can see how easy it is to zip files on iPadOS, and unzipping them is even simpler.

- Launch the Files app and go to the zipped file you want to unzip.
- Click on the file.
- The file will then unzip and turn into a folder within that same folder. Click to access the contents.

Scan Documents from the Files App

- Launch the Files app on your iPad
- Touch the **Browse** tab at the bottom of the Files app.
- Touch the **More** button (three-dot icon) at the top of the display.

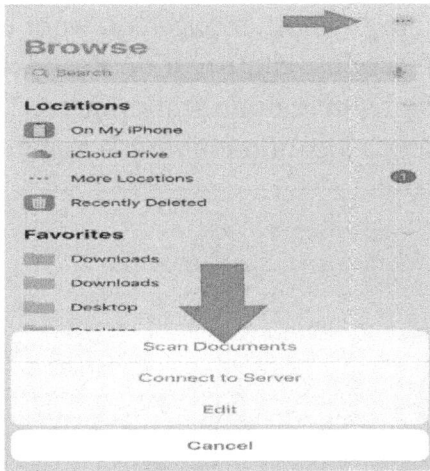

- Touch **Scan Documents**.
- Place your document in the viewer and touch the Capture button.
- You can decide to drag the corners to modify it, touch to **Retake** or touch to **Keep Scan**.

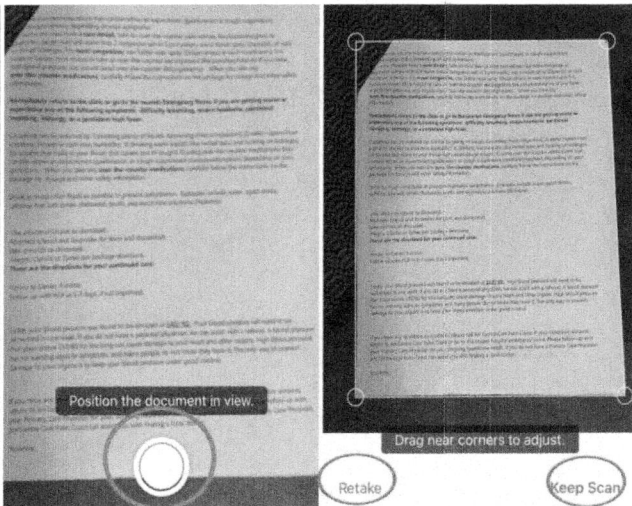

- If there's another page you want to scan, you can just capture it on the next screen.
- When you're done scanning, tap "**Save**."
- Select a location for your scan and touch "**Save**."

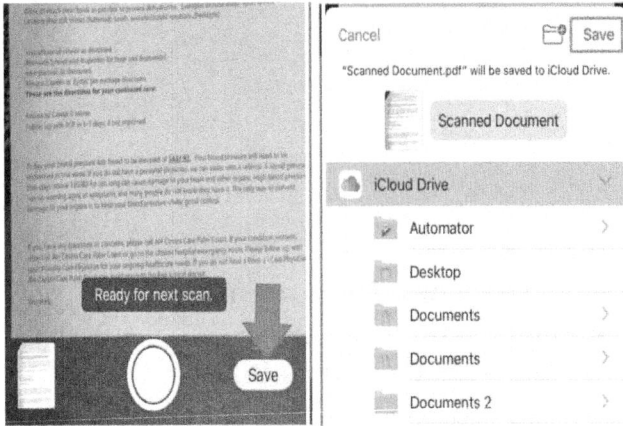

- You can also scan a document within a location like iCloud Drive or On My iPad in the Files app.
- Tap the **More** button (three-dot icon) at the upper left and then follow the same steps above.

How to Apply Filter to Video

- Open the stock Photos app on your iPad.

- Choose a video from your Photo collection using the Photos tab.
- Once you've chosen a video, tap **Edit** in the upper right corner of the screen.

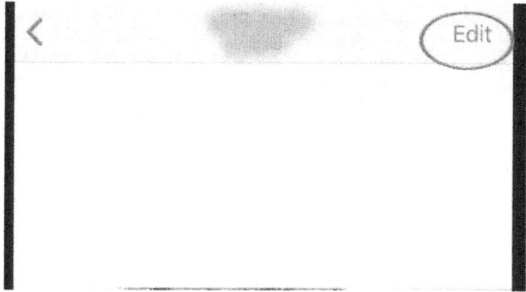

- Tap the **filter** icon (appears like a Venn drawing) at the lower part of the screen.

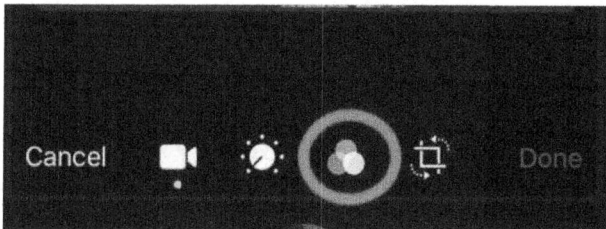

- Swipe through the nine accessible filters to get a preview of every one applied to your video.
- Rest your finger, and a horizontal dial will appear underneath the chosen filter. Use your finger to move the dial and alter the intensity level of the filter.
- Tap "**Done**" at the bottom right of the display to apply the filter effect to your video.

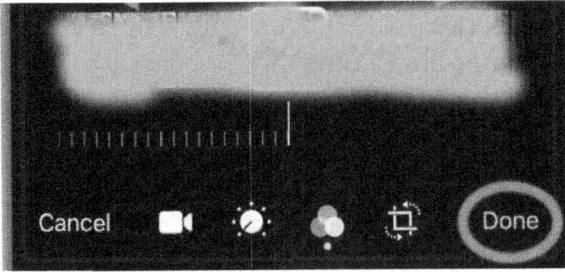

Note: You can apply these filters at whatever point you capture videos via the Camera app.

- Open the stock Photos app.
- Open the Photos app
- Choose a Portrait photo in your Photo library. If it isn't a recent Portrait photo that you want to edit, you can use the Days, Months, and Years views to whittle down your collection.
- Check the image was captured in Portrait mode by looking for the Portrait label in the top-left corner of the screen, then tap **Edit** in the top-right corner to enter the editing interface.

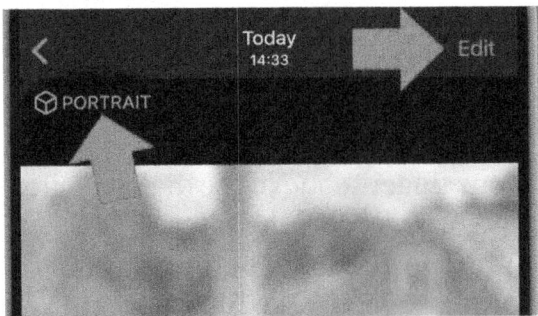

- With the Portrait icon selected in the bottom row of tools, select a lighting mode by sliding your finger along the icons below the photo.

- Once a lighting mode is selected, such as the new High-Key Light Mono effect (shown), you'll see a slider appear below it. Move your fingertip along it to dial down or ratchet up the intensity of the lighting effect.

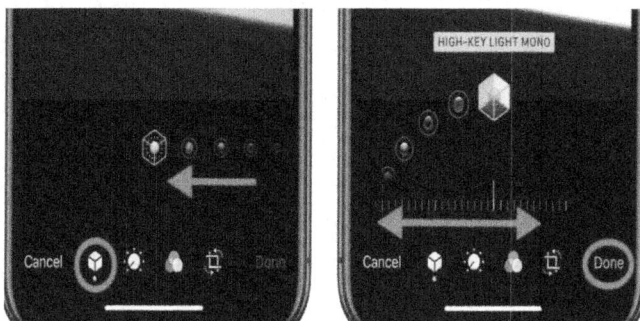

- Tap "**Done**" when you're happy with how the image looks.

Save and Share Webpage as a PDF

- Launch the Safari app on your iPad and visit any web page of your choice and let the page get loaded completely, else, it will not be able to save full page as PDF later on.
- Now press and hold the Home button and Side button at once to capture a screenshot on your iPad in Safari.

137

- You can now see the preview of the screenshot taken on the bottom left corner, tap on the screenshot and then tap on **Full Page** option that's available on the right top corner.

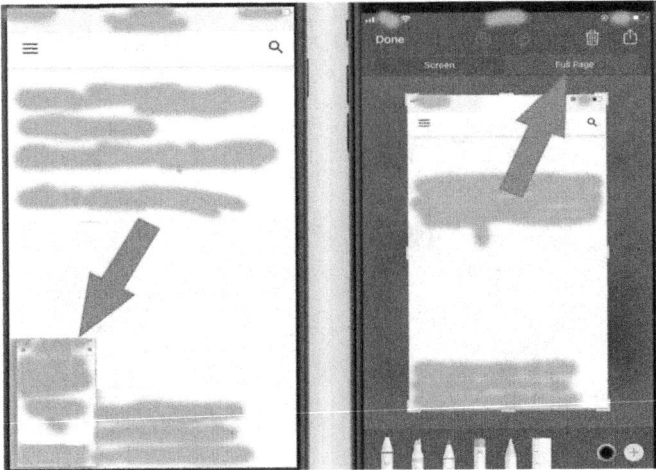

- Next, tap on "**Done**" and then select **Save PDF to Files**" option.

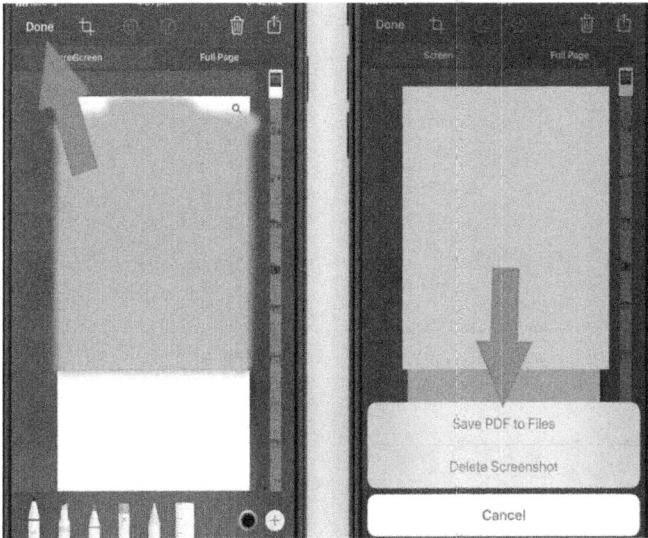

- Select any of the folders from "**On My iPad**" or "**iCloud Drive**". If the desired folder isn't available, create one and then tap on "**Save.**" This will save your PDF.

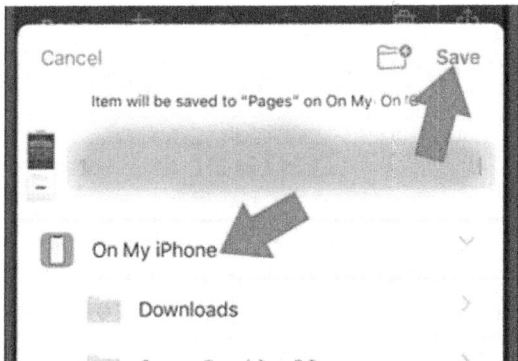

- If you want to share the PDF via Email or iMessage, after the third step, tap on the share button option available on the top right corner.

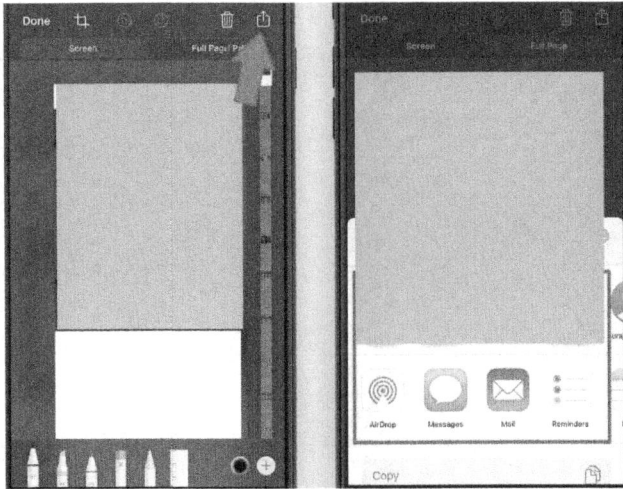

- Once done, select iMessage/Mail or any other platform, enter the recipient, and tap on "**Send**." That's it!

Enable Content Blockers in Safari

Content blockers offer a one-trick solution for prohibiting ads like popups and banners from stacking on websites you visit. They can likewise shield you from online tracking by deactivating cookies and scripts that sites try to load.

- Open the **Settings** app.
- Scroll down and tap **Safari**.
- Under **General**, touch **Content Blockers**.

- To activate content blockers, flip the switches to the ON position.

Note: Content Blockers option doesn't appear in Safari's settings until you've installed a third-party content blocker from the App Store.

Temporarily Disable Content Blockers in Safari

- Open Safari on your iPad and go to the site in question.
- Tap the "**aA**" icon in the upper left corner of the screen to uncover the **Website View** menu.
- Tap **Turn Off Content Blockers**.
- If you only need to disable content blockers for a particular website, tap **Website Settings** in the **Website View** menu, and afterward flip the switch next to **Use Content Blockers** to the OFF position.

Access the Download Manager in Safari

- When you try to download a file on Safari, a little download icon is displayed in the upper right corner of the screen.
- You can tap the icon to check the status of your downloads, and tapping the magnifying glass next to the file will open its folder location.
- By default, files downloaded in Safari are stored in the "**Downloads**" section of the Files app. However, you can customize the storage location: go to the **Settings** app, select the **Safari** section, and tap **Downloads**. From this screen, you can select to store downloaded files in **iCloud Drive**, on your **iPad**, or in another location based on your personal preference.
- The Downloads screen in Safari settings has an option to "Remove download list items automatically after one day" (the default), "Upon successful download," or "Manually."

Change the Default Safari Download Location

- Open the **Settings** app
- Tap **Safari**
- Select **Downloads**. You would then be able to choose one of the recommended places or tap "**Other**" to pick another registry. Third-party apps might have the option to support this, so if your favored location is turned gray out, you may need to hang tight for a future app update.

How to Automatically Close All Open Safari Tabs

- Launch the **Settings** app.
- Scroll down and tap **Safari**.
- Locate the section tagged "**Tabs**" and select "**Close Tabs**."
- The default will be manual. Select the timeframe you want your tabs to close automatically.

Manually: Safari won't automatically close tabs.

After One Day: All open tabs will be cleared after 24 hours.

After One Week: All open tabs will be cleared in seven days' time.

After One Month: All open tabs will be cleared following a month.

Enable/Disable Limit Ad Tracking

- Launch the **Settings** app
- Tap **Privacy**.
- Find the **Advertising** option situated at the bottom of the page, and then search for the **Limit Ad Tracking** option.
- Flip the **Limit Ad Tracking** option to on or off base on preference.
- It ought to be noticed that you can generally re-enable ad tracking by following the means above, yet flipping the relevant options on by tapping them to turn them green (on account of location-based tracking) and dark (for Limit Ad Tracking).

Turn On Voice Control

- Go to **Settings**.

- Touch **Accessibility**.
- Touch **Voice Control**.
- Switch Voice Control on. Since Voice Control is active, you'll see a blue microphone icon appear alongside the clock in the top left. This means Voice Control is on and continually tuning in for commands.
- Now, you can begin utilizing Voice Control; you presumably don't realize what commands are accessible to you. For an outline of what you can say and do, tap **Customize Commands**. There are many, numerous commands, and they're each split up into classifications. Tapping one will show all of you the acknowledged phrases that will trigger a particular action.
- You can likewise include commands, utilizing the **Create New Commands** option inside the **Customize Commands** page. To create a command Voice Control will notice, you'll need to indicate the type of the action and the application where it is to be used before you work out the command itself.
- If you only need Voice Control to listen when you're staring at your device, switch on the Attention Aware setting on the main Voice Control screen. At the point when your device notices you're not staring any longer it, Voice Control will be switched to sleep; however, to use Voice Control without staring at your device,

you'll need to say "Wake Up" before proceeding to your command.

- All things considered, there are two commands specifically you should be open to using: "Show Grid" and "Show Numbers." These commands will enable you to connect with anything on your iPad's screen, regardless of whether there's no default phrase for what you're attempting to perform with Voice Control.

How to Block Email Senders

- To do this, first, make sure that the email address you want to block is linked to a contact in your device
- Then block that contact by tapping on their name and selecting **Block this Caller**.
- Next, open the Settings app and tap **Mail**.
- Under the Threading header, tap **Blocked Sender Options**, then tap **Move to Trash**.

How to Unblock a Number on iPad

- Go to **Settings** > **Phone** or launch **Settings** > **FaceTime**.
- Touch Call Blocking & Identification.
- While on the **Blocked Contacts** list, swipe right to left through the number, then touch **Unblock**.

Unblock People Who Text You

- If you had blocked someone in Messages, you could unblock the number in the Messages app to enable them to text you again.
- Go to **Settings**
- Tap **Messages**.
- Scroll down and tap **Blocked**.
- Swipe from right to left on the number you wish to unblock and then tap **Unblock**.

How to Add Contacts on iPad

- Launch the Phone app.
- Touch **Contacts**.
- Touch the"+" icon situated at the top right-hand corner of the display.
- Input the details into the fields for the First Name and Last Name, respectively.
- Tap on **Add Phone**, and afterward enter the contact phone number.
- Tap on **Add Email**, and afterward type in the contact email address.
- Touch "**Done**" to save.
- Navigate or search the name on the Contacts to check if it was effectively saved. If you wish to add more contacts, simply follow the same process.

Set Up Voicemail

- Launch the Phone app. At the bottom of the device window, you will see the Voicemail icon in the right corner. Select it to open up your visual voicemail.
- The voicemail screen should show a blank space with a button to Set up now in the middle of the screen. Select this. If you have used iPad's voicemail service

previously, you can sign in with your old password here to automatically access your old voicemails. If you have never made use of visual voicemail, you should create a password and re-enter it. Whenever completed, select "**Done**."

- Now your iPad will show the Greeting screen. If you don't fancy the greeting, you can choose Default and afterward "**Done**" to skip this part. If you need to personalize your greeting, select **Custom**, and then **Record** to record your greeting and **Play** to repeat it. When you're happy with it, select "**Done**."
- Your iPad voicemail is currently officially set up.

How to Merge Duplicate Contacts

- To merge duplicate contacts, simply open a contact and tap on the "**Edit**" button.
- Next, select the "**Link contacts**" option. This will open your contacts list. Simply select the contacts you wish to merge with the current one. That's all!

Copy Contacts from Social Networks & Email

- Launch the Settings app.
- Tap **Passwords & Accounts**.
- Choose a social network or an email account
- Touch the pointer next to "**Contacts**" to turn on the function.
- Slide your finger upwards, beginning from the bottom of the screen to go to the home screen.

Set Up Emergency Medical ID

- Open the **Health** app
- Touch "**Medical ID**" at the bottom-right corner
- Next, tap on "**Create Medical ID**" to start adding your health info.
- On the following screen, enter all your medical information, including allergies, well-being conditions, emergency contact details, and any helpful notes. This will be valuable if there's an occurrence of an emergency, and anyone around you can rapidly access this information.

- After you are done with adding the details, switch ON "**Show When Locked**." This feature is optional yet exceptionally recommended. The reason is that all the info you have entered will be noticeable to others regardless of whether your iPad is encrypted.
- That is all; you would now be able to leave the Health app and lock your iPad. You can confirm whether it is working or not by swiping up to the Passcode screen and afterward tapping on **Emergency** and then tap on **Medical ID**.

CONCLUSION

The iPad Pro is a great device with lots of new features in the new iPadOS you'll definitely enjoy having this gadget. It is my concern to teach you how to use your devices in an easy and understandable way without bluffing, and I hope you're satisfied with my level of input. I made this for you and presumable you can now do everything about the iPad Pro. I hope you find this guide useful and insightful, and it has helped you to find solutions to the most important features you ever wanted. Good luck and cheers.

ABOUT AUTHOR

Aaron Madison is a computer jerk, researcher, and a gadget perfectionist who loves to have all the latest gadgets. He loves to teach people how to use their devices and maximize its potential; He knows how to satisfy gadgets freaks and where to look to satisfy the teeming number of tech lovers. Aaron likes teaching the most complicated of things and making it simple for users. Aaron always gives you an "awe "feeling. You have no option but to love him when he writes as he includes all the necessary details and information.

Other books by the Author

1. iPhone 11 Series Tips & Tricks User Guide

https://amzn.to/34RaszQ

2. Apple Watch Series 5 User Guide For
    Beginners & Seniors

https://amzn.to/32yKqzO

3. MacBook Pro User Guide for New Users &
    Seniors

https://amzn.to/2Czy7sg

4. MacBook Air (2019) User Guide for
    Beginners & Seniors

https://amzn.to/33OBXcU

5. macOS Catalina User Guide

https://amzn.to/2XdwXMR

6. Samsung Galaxy S10, S10 Plus & S10e
    User's Guide

https://amzn.to/2CG2soY

Made in the USA
Coppell, TX
06 August 2020